PERSONAL SOCRATES

Questions That Will Upgrade Your Life
From Legends & World-Class Performers

Marc Champagne

BARONFIG

BARONFIG CIRCUS BOOKS

An imprint of Baronfig Inc., New York City
baronfig.com

Text © 2021 by Marc Champagne
Design © 2021 by Baronfig Inc.
Exterior & interior design by Joey Cofone
Printed in Taiwan

First Edition - First Print
ISBN: 978-1-943623-35-8

To my wife Roxanne and son Caleb, your energy,
support, and love made this book possible.

To the hundreds of stunning humans I have
interviewed and the world-class performers and
legends featured in the pages to come.

Contents

Contents

Contents

Introduction

I SAT ALONE IN SILENCE. My eyes fixated on my laptop screen displaying the Apple metrics from KYO, the digital journaling app and mental fitness company I had cofounded three and a half years prior. It was the idea that made me leave a well-paying job, a comfortable environment, and a secure life. As I glanced over the screen, one number made me shake my head in wonder—86,997,014. The number of people we had reached in just under two years of being in the App Store. My next move was to hit the "delete app from App Store" button.

Despite all the hype in the media, collaborations with respected brands, and app features from Apple all around the world, KYO was failing. We needed more time and resources to develop a sustainable business model, and we no longer had either.

After hitting "delete" a flurry of questions passed through my mind like a rocket with no chance of returning to earth. How does this make sense? How could I fail at such a colossal level? What would people think? What judgments would people have? What would our investors and advisors say? As my chest tightened with anxiety, I remember feeling like a broken human that not only let himself down but also his family.

I had uprooted my wife and one-year-old son, Caleb, from the neighborhood, city, and home we loved in Montreal to move to Toronto, with the idea of being in Canada's largest city to seize opportunity for the business while also being physically closer to my cofounder. Living in Toronto came with prospects, but it also came with a much higher cost of living. However, that was okay because we sold our condo in Montreal and would rent a home for a year until the business took off, then we could find the ideal neighborhood and home to raise our family.

At the time, the business plan and financials backed up the decision to relocate. I would have regretted not relocating and giving the idea all my energy and the best chance to succeed. Despite how the business turned out, taking that opportunity led to the most impactful self-development years of my life to date.

The worst part was the temporary destruction of my mind from deleting the app. I was not just deleting an app from the store: I was deleting my identity from the last three years, the motivation surrounding a new idea, and any hopes of helping millions of people—with one action from my finger on my touchpad. At least this is what I was hearing from my internal narrative.

I never felt more alone in my life than at that moment. The business had financially failed. My backup plan of returning to the industry I had left behind to pursue this app idea no longer felt aligned with what I wanted in my life. I was living in a house that I hated and could not even afford. Every morning, I physically felt sick and struggled to recognize the face I saw in the mirror.

I was also terrified that my now three-year-old would pick up on the extreme stress in our household and be scarred later in life. The worst part: for the first time in my life, I had no plan forward because of crippling fear.

The Turning Point

In my darkest days, I turned to journaling, and the detail with which I interrogated myself led to a critical realization and the foundation for this book: *at any point, we are one question away from a different life.* It took time, but each day, I resorted back to my mental fitness—training for my mind to process emotion, be more clear, and live each day with intention.

The training came from all the practices, insights, and key learnings from years of soaking up knowledge from books, blogs, podcasts, and the reflective questions I had gathered from interviewing hundreds of brilliant humans over the years through multiple podcasts, including the show I still host today: Behind The Human.

I physically and mentally slowed down by harnessing the present moment to absorb and study exceptional people's minds. I took their wisdom and flipped it into reflective questions allowing me to think about where and how I could apply that wisdom to my current situation. The questions were critical because without them the wisdom often only served as short bursts of inspiration versus the clarity and sustainable motivation I needed to reignite my mind. The journaling allowed me to go deeper through and apply what I was learning in real time.

Perhaps the most significant and most valuable shift showed up in the type of questions I was asking. I went from destructive and shaming questions like, "What would people think?" to curiosity-driven and empowering questions, like the prompts you are about to experience in the profiles to come, such as, "What would make today great?"

Each day provided micro-moments of reflection and clarity leading up to living with purpose and intention. Now was the time for radical honesty—no filters, just me, the page, and the biggest question of them all: What do I want for my life? This question changed everything for me. It brought back hope, excitement, and started the process of creating a plan. One question led to the next, and the next one after that, until the steps forward were clear and felt right: a process I now know as the Socratic method.

Spending time with powerful questions, like many historical figures before me, allowed me to learn from the past, build myself back up, and have a clear vision for where I was heading. Seeing the power of a single prompt, I knew I had to unlock this practice for more people, but from a different perspective, through the narrative of the questions shaping the lives of extraordinary humans. Stories that would be relatable and meet people specifically where they were in their journey. Without those few minutes of reflection each day and well-timed questions from people I could relate to, I would have easily slipped into a dark depression.

When we are clear and act with intention and purpose, we expand what is possible. Now, I'm going to help you find the question(s) that will unlock more clarity and intention in your life.

The Power of Questions

A great question forces us to think, and think hard. A great question leads to other questions and ultimately to the answers we are seeking. It takes work, consistency, and motivation to stay the course; but when we do, the opportunities are exponential for us and everyone around us.

Each of the sections that follow will help you understand the questions behind exceptional humans' thinking—from the past and the present. After studying the minds of many, I have realized that questions are a universal language not shaped by time. Even though time, history, and circumstances surrounding a question may be different, the outcomes are the same: more clarity, insight, and confidence in processing our thoughts and decisions.

Every aspect of this book will evolve as your life does. Questions that resonate today may not resonate tomorrow and vice versa. Please take what you need in the present moment, but always know you have the wisdom and guiding prompts of brilliant minds whenever life calls for them. You are priming your mind to thrive each day as you continue to exercise and train your "curiosity muscles" at the same level as the guests and reflective system within these pages.

The Socratic Method

In my personal story I shared how one question changed my life: What do I want for my life? This prompt was the starting point, the big question so to speak, to bring clarity to a foggy mind. One question led to others, and others after that until I felt like I had reached the core of what I truly wanted in my life. The more questions I asked, the more I could go past the surface and progress toward the clarity I was seeking.

It turns out there is a method to this line of questioning: the

Socratic method. I was writing this book with the desire to understand and catalogue the questions shaping the minds and lives of top-performing humans in order for us all to reflect with the greats, perform at our best, and feel great doing so.

As I continued down the path of understanding what this book was, a system or process to upgrade my reflective process kept surfacing. The Socratic method is designed to break a challenge down into a series of questions that eventually will provide the answers we seek. It is a technique that has stood the test of time, having originated between 469-399 BC.

As I explained my reflective system powered by questions to Joey Cofone, CEO of Baronfig (also the publisher of this book) he naturally said, "This is the Socratic method," where I replied, "Socratic what?"

My curiosity was sparked, and I needed to understand how Socrates so many centuries ago developed a reflective method that shaped my entire life, and many others' lives, without us being conscious of the method. In addition, I needed to understand how a flow of questions could prevent me from slipping into a deep depression, but instead, propel my life forward.

Perhaps the question that intrigued me the most was: How could I modernize the method to be approachable, applicable, and relatable to people of today? And not just for people, like Joey, who have studied literature and philosophy.

We all ask questions, but are they the right ones, the best ones, and are we asking enough of them? The answers to these questions will all surface as you navigate through the profiles of this book. Let Kobe Bryant, Jane Austen, Ryan Holiday, and all the other stunning humans be our guides to uncovering a different way to think.

Most know of the scholar, teacher, and philosopher Socrates, yet many have no idea of the Socratic method—the same method fuelling the reflection of each guest featured in the pages to come.

> *"I cannot teach anyone anything. I can*
> *only make them think." —Socrates*

Many have written about Socrates, including his students, most notably Plato. They all presented slightly different views of his character. Still, his overall lifestyle was consistently portrayed to not convey knowledge, but to "rather [ask] question after clarifying question until his students arrived at their own understanding." For example, using a question like, "What exactly does this mean?" to clarify his students' thinking and understanding of an argument.

Through the profiles, you will experience many clarifying questions like, "What is my art reflecting?" from Pablo Picasso, or "What discomfort am I running from?" from Chris Messina, inventor of the hashtag. Each prompt and profile is designed to spark reflection by starting with a "big question" followed by further unpacking the topic to bring more clarity, intentionality, and possibility to your life.

Scholars of Socrates have noted six types of questions forming the basis of the Socratic method:

1. **Clarifying thinking:** Questions to stimulate deeper thought and increase understanding (What is my art reflecting? Pablo Picasso)
2. **Probing assumptions:** Questions to help see another

path (How do I become irreplaceable? Coco Chanel)

3. **Probing rationale:** Questions that help support reason and evidence (What is within my control? Ryan Holiday)

4. **Challenging perspectives:** Questions to open up different points of view (What if it were possible? Naveen Jain)

5. **Probing implications:** Questions to think logically about outcomes (Who am I optimizing to become? James Clear)

6. **Questioning the question:** Questions to understand what's truly behind a behavior (What discomfort am I running from? Chris Messina)

I understood the question types but wanted to develop a simpler grouping that we could quickly and intuitively recall to guide our reflection. So, I have grouped the question types into three categories, which also led to this book's structure:

1. Getting clear
2. Living intentionally
3. Expanding possibility

When I was following this structure to write each profile, it was a pleasurable experience. The writing just flowed, but when I tried to shortcut the phases outlined above, it got painful. For example, if I tried to write a profile while still in the "getting clear" step, I felt lost, scattered, and I did not know where to go with the writing. I started to doubt the value of the profile, my writing, and my interpretation of the person inspiring the prompts. This led to more doubt, bigger doubt if you will, firing up looping narratives around the overall value of the book and wondering if any of you would actually find the book useful. Is this sequence of thoughts starting to sound familiar?

The self-doubt that arises from one event leads to more looping thoughts, doubt, and eventually a halt in our progress. We are not the first and not the last to go through this experience, but we all can pause and redirect the cycle to better serve us. The method and sequence of reflection used throughout the book works for any and all situations, thoughts, and emotions. Let the stories and prompts from the profiles guide you no matter where you may be in life.

When I focused on doing the research to feel clear in my mind, a one-page intentional outline appeared with greater ease, leading to an expansion of possibility through the words landing on the page that only minutes before did not exist. I can say with confidence, I know you will find value through the words, prompts, and system of reflection presented in the pages to come.

Socrates left us all a beautiful gift, a method of reflection through questions. This method pulled my life out of a downward-trending tailspin and now allows me to reflect like the greats and expand possibility. Using the prompts and mental fitness practices detailed in the following pages is like having your very own Personal Socrates with you at all times, a tool and method that can be used in any situation to bring clarity, intentionality, and possibility to every aspect of your life.

Getting the Most Out of This Book

Outside of reading the introduction in one sitting, I encourage taking in the rest of the book slowly. Select one profile each morning to prime your mind, inspire your reflection, and practice mental fitness training. Skim the profiles and let your intuition make the selection. In many cases, there are reasons why your fingers will stop on a specific page. Follow the signs and see where the path takes you.

I wrote these profiles to offer high-value reflective moments within the shortest amount of time in order to easily integrate them within your current mental fitness routine, or to become your mental fitness routine. Each profile will exercise your mind, stimulate thought, and offer different perspectives to consistently prime your mind at elite levels.

It is important to note that the profiles are not memoirs or biographies, but reflections inspired by the subject's wisdom leaving you with prompts to upgrade your reflection and thinking. Just as I prepare for any podcast interview, I do a certain level of research that allows me to feel confident going into the conversation, and in this case, write a profile.

I intend to stimulate unique reflection, and have resisted stifling the process with too much historical detail. There are many great authors and biographers before me who have already mastered those memoirs and biographies. The magic exists in our interpretation of the legends and top performers with where we are in our lives right now. Therefore, the most significant gift you can give yourself while consuming this book is to interact with the content. There are countless wellness and mental fitness practices profiled along with the reflective questions. Journal on the prompts that resonate most with you in the present moment; write directly in the book, use note-taking apps, or write in your favorite notebook.

As said by Socrates, "Knowledge is our ultimate good." I challenge you to apply that knowledge within the context of your own life and experiences.

Working Through Specific Challenges

We all learn and grow from processing challenging situations or by navigating the curve balls life throws at us. Chances are, those profiled in this book have also processed similar situations. Even though no two situations are the same, the practices and prompts in these profiles can be applied in many circumstances. Drop in with a specific challenge and let the prompts and your mind do the rest!

Have Fun and Experiment

Remember, just because one person may not enjoy running doesn't mean that exercise is not for them. The same principle applies to mental fitness. Experiment with different practices, answer the questions that seem most daunting, and enjoy the mental expansion that accompanies these experiences. It's okay if you don't want to hear the answer to a particular prompt or you sense fear that may surface. Often what we fear most is exactly where we should begin.

I was terrified after my reflection revealed that my back-up plan of returning to my corporate career no longer felt aligned with what I wanted for my life. Suddenly, the sense of security, safety, and comfort in knowing I had a back-up plan dissolved. That was scary, but I also felt empowered because I was clear in what felt right: learning from the best in the world to then guide others through impactful reflection and mental fitness.

As you read through the book, please be kind to yourself. The act of reflecting on powerful questions is a practice; and like any practice, it can be awkward at first and will take time to settle in, but it will get easier with time and consistency. I can promise one thing with 100% certainty—when you upgrade your questions, you upgrade your life. Thank you for being here, for being curious, and for prioritizing your mind. We all win when your mind is healthy, clear, and motivated.

Introduction

PART ONE

Get Clear

Think of your mind as a stunning library with large windows casting light onto books spanning floor to ceiling within neatly organized rows. Any knowledge you seek is available at your fingertips.

Okay, so now let's get real. Our mental libraries most likely do not look like this. The looping thoughts, narratives, relationships, and emotions that we all experience are like tipping over the bookshelves, forcing us to rummage through piles of books to find the information and answers we seek.

Just as we can clean up and organize a physical space, we can do the same within our minds. The brilliant humans in this section have leveraged mental fitness to train and maintain clear mental pathways. We have access to this same training. Let the prompts within each profile guide you in creating clearer mental space. When we create space in our minds through reflection, we allow clarity to surface. We can now see signs that were always there but might have been hidden or masked by other factors. No matter the situation, getting clear will always unlock a path forward.

How can I ask the most powerful questions?

Cal Fussman

Iconic journalist, author, and storyteller

QUICK BIO

- Longtime writer for *Esquire* magazine and *New York Times* best-selling author
- Interviewed icons like Muhammad Ali, Serena Williams, Jeff Bezos, Robert DeNiro, presidents, and essentially any other legend you can think of
- Host of the *Big Questions* podcast (iTunes top 50 show)
- Had breakfast with Larry King each morning
- Philosophy to life: If you change your questions, you can change your life.
- One of the greatest interviewers and storytellers of all time

---

Behind the Question

Cal Fussman asks some of the most thoughtful, well-timed, and impactful questions I have ever heard. Sometimes you don't even realize the question has been asked because as the listener you are engrossed in every detail he pulls out of the person on the other side of the microphone. I am stunned every time I witness his talent, and not surprisingly, he's interviewed the most significant humans of our time.

I remember my heart racing, sitting in front of my microphone, waiting for Cal to appear on my screen. Now I was asking the questions and hearing the voice of a legend reply in what I can only describe as a poetic storyteller. I would ask my question, then do the only thing I should be doing: mute the mic, shut up, and listen to Cal's words. I was not taking notes, and I was not thinking of the next question. I was just listening and allowing the conversation to flow, something I learned from Cal.

Before we can understand how to ask the most powerful questions, we need to understand what was behind the most critical question (in my opinion) Cal has ever asked. It was the question that sparked a response from President Lyndon B. Johnson when Cal was only a seven-year-old boy. This question unlocked an understanding of what one question could do.

At that time, President Kennedy had just been shot, and the United States, along with much of the world, had been left in shock with many questions of their own. Cal was no different. For the first time in his life he was confronting death. His parents sat him down to explain everything was going to be all right. The White House had plans for events like this, and over time life would go back to normal. It took time, and his parents were right, but Cal was still left pondering who Lyndon B. Johnson was and what he was thinking after being defaulted to the seat of the president from a horrific event. Was he happy, sad, or scared? He picked up a pencil and asked a question that would turn out to be one of the most significant moments of his life.

"Dear President Johnson—how does it feel to be president?"

What happened next opened Cal's mind to the power of a question. Months later, his mother raced up the stairs with a letter addressed to Cal from the White House. This fixated everyone—family, friends, school teachers, and principals. Everyone wanted to see the letter. At that moment, Cal realized that "the smallest kid in the second-grade class suddenly became a big man."

He was touched in a way that would forge a path of lifelong curiosity because Cal was taught that a single question could get you to the most powerful person on earth. This curiosity has stayed with Cal and turned him into an iconic interviewer. As he stated, "There was no ambition behind this, it's not like I wanted a seat in the cabinet one day. I just wanted to know how it felt to be Lyndon B. Johnson. And, I'm sure there were a lot of other people who wanted to know what it felt like." What separated Cal from the others is he wrote that question down, put it in an envelope, and mailed it off to be answered.

What questions are you *not* asking?

Cal took the action that many did not—he asked the questions that were on his mind. There is nothing complicated about the process besides understanding what might be holding us back. If we don't ask, we don't receive. So, from a place of genuine curiosity, let's start asking!

We get blocked from asking great questions when we overthink the situation. This happens all the time—in meetings, interviews, and conversations—when trying to focus on figuring out the best angle or the best question to unlock the next one. When operating from this perspective we are running our own agenda and removing any chance of the magic from surfacing which comes from listening and being present in the moment.

Cal's preparation for an interview is remarkable, yet straightforward and incredibly useful. I've adopted his approach in my own preparation for interviews. I have since realized that his system can be used in many situations—not only for interviews, but in any situation where a conversation is involved.

Try this: List every question that comes to mind when preparing for a conversation. No filter, no limit. If you're researching something or someone, keep writing out the questions as they naturally arise. Hundreds of questions will surface, just as Cal experiences before going into an interview with someone like Robert De Niro or Muhammad Ali. The next step is not as intuitive. Cal picks up the sheet of paper and rips it up. Now he's ready for the interview.

Wait, what?

Hold your gasps now because you're probably making the correct assumption: Does Cal go into his interviews without questions or a pad of paper in front of him? Sort of. Physically he has no questions in front of him, but mentally, he has them all. Don't worry, he's not superhuman, and we can all do this by going through the exercise detailed above while trusting our mind to do the rest.

Cal's curiosity primes his mind by presenting the questions he may ask. He goes into the interview, trusting his mind will surface the right question at the right time based on the flow of conversation. He can only do this if he's truly present in the discussion, not scribbling down notes or thinking of the next question while the other person is still speaking.

Does this sound familiar? You do not have to be a writer for *Esquire* or be a podcast host to resonate with this situation. Any meeting, conversation, phone call, or video chat can set up the same problem—a lack of presence. You can get by in these situations, and many do, but you will never connect with the other person in a way that causes them to open up and lean in. When you enter a conversation confident in your research and fully present with the person in front of you, the best questions will surface. These are the questions that *should* be asked, but might have been the questions you were *not* asking in the past.

How can I wake up with answers?

You might assume the master of questions always has the answers. Surprise! Cal is human like the rest of us, but he does have a great method to get to the answers when they might not be initially apparent. He has written countless stories, but never starts writing with a blank mind.

In an interview with poet IN-Q (stage name of Adam Schmalholz), Cal shared, "You need the starting point to write." If he doesn't have that starting point, Cal goes to sleep. But, he goes to sleep with a question: What do I want to say? When he wakes up, he has the answer to that question and the words start to flow. You don't have to be a writer to use this technique. We often underestimate the power of our minds. We have many answers or solutions to the problems we are trying to solve if we let our minds make the connections. When we are sleeping, we do not have all the distractions or noise of the day; therefore, our mind can pull from our knowledge bank and start forming the necessary connections.

Write your question before going to sleep. Upon waking, go straight to that notebook and answer the question. I am always amazed at what surfaces on the page when eight hours before there was nothing. Try it out!

Cal Fussman is fully present in an interview knowing that

the hundreds of questions he's ripped up from his research will surface at the right moment. Cal trusts the power of his mind, and so can we.

Final Thought

You will never get an answer to a question you don't ask.

What does it mean to be unapologetically me?

Robin Williams

Actor, comedian, and improvisational master

July 21, 1951 – August 11, 2014

QUICK BIO

- Best known for his fast-paced improvisational performances
- Regarded as one of the best comedians of all time with a talent so unique that few could even attempt to copy it
- Nominated for four Academy Awards, winning Best Supporting Actor for his role in *Good Will Hunting*
- Garnered several other accolades, including two Primetime Emmy Awards, six Golden Globe Awards, two Screen Actors Guild Awards, and five Grammy Awards

---

Behind the Question

Whether it be in person, behind the screen, or through audio, experiencing Robin Wiliams was always the same: electric, playful, and unapologetically himself.

As Robin was cast to lead in his first TV series, *Mork & Mindy,* the industry standard of three cameras required to film a TV series was not enough to capture Robin in action. For the first time, a fourth camera was added to follow Robin as he flew back and forth across the set. This was Robin Williams: a person who always left us wondering what was happening behind the scenes of his mind to put on a performance like no other.

Robin once said, "The world is open for play." He operated from within with no rules, limits, or filters. On stage, he allowed his imagination to run free and express who he was while transporting his audience into a world free of worry and stress, and fuelled by laughter, joy, and the present moment.

Robin's performances seemed unattainable to the average person, but in fact, what was behind his remarkable performances goes back to something we all have access to—the present moment. "If you just relax, listen, and be in the scene, you won't have to worry about finding the funny line." Robin went on to further explain the importance of not interfering with yourself, "If you don't do anything, you'll be amazed at how much you're doing."

Tapping into the present moment is all about listening and feeling the moment you are in, allowing the moment to guide you and bring you on a journey. Mental fitness practices, such as journaling on the prompts within these profiles, are fantastic ways to boost self-awareness, allowing us to tap into the present moment more easily.

Robin crafted this skill early on as a child through his imagination. Growing up as an only child, he kept himself entertained while his parents were away for extended periods on business. Many years later, his ability to fully access the present moment and allow his imagination to take him and his audience into another world would make Robin the legend we all remember.

There is only one Robin Williams, just like we are uniquely our own person. Therefore, it's not about replicating Robin, but understanding how he harnessed his imagination, sense of play, and the present moment to apply these skills to our own lives. Being on stage, feeding off others' energy, and genuinely listening from within was the playground allowing Robin to be unapologetically himself.

I invite you to reflect on what makes you unapologetically you and how your playground is either supporting you or pushing you away from being you. As mentioned by Robin in relation to performing stand-up comedy, or his playground, "When it works, it's great; when it doesn't, it's painful." Think of the elements and environment to make it work for you. Reflect on what you might be hiding away or what you would love to share with this world if there were no fear of judgement or failure to hold you back.

We can use a page and a pen to start releasing our internal narrative of fear and share what was meant to be shared. Take your time, but as you get comfortable expressing the true you to yourself, it will become easier to take the next step in expressing it to others. Stepping into who we are, stripping away our masks or shields, can be scary. We may feel different from everyone else and what is expected of us by society, but think of how freeing it will feel when we strip away the fear and, as Robin would say, step into the world to play.

How do I rechannel the fear that comes with being me?

There were two Robin Williamses: one we experienced on stage who was free and limitless and the other who had the same fears and narratives of self-doubt that we all experience. The scale and circumstances for Robin might have been different, but the emotions were precisely the same. He used his craft to navigate through his emotions, or as he once said, "Stand-up was a great survival mechanism."

Those closest to him would hint that this strategy was merely a crutch to keep himself going, and in fact it only temporarily buried his internal narrative. As mentioned by Steve Martin, "On stage, he was the master, in charge, and quick—but in life, he was less comfortable off stage." I share these two sides of Robin because most people, myself included, only knew the external-facing persona. In reality, someone at the top of their game has to process the same emotions we all face.

Being unapologetically the person we want to be can push us to the edge, where emotions are often overpowering. We have a critical decision to make: to ignore them, or like Robin, rechannel them to the stage and fuel our work, passion, and life. How do we do this? Recognizing what we fear and where it is showing up in our lives is a great place to start. Feelings of uncertainty, anxiety, and dread are great clues to pinpointing our fear.

Try this: In one short sentence, list out what you fear. Beside each sentence, note what is behind that fear or what is fuelling it. Step outside of your emotional mind and step into rational thinking. (Make sure to explore Dan Doty's profile for specific somatic techniques to help disconnect our emotional minds.) Our fears are often being fuelled by fictitious internal narratives. Let's cut the fuel, work with the facts, focus only on what we can control, and rechannel the fear.

One effective fear-rechanneling technique I've found helpful is to dictate how I want to feel after a particular situation. For example, whenever I feel fear and anxiety arise before a difficult conversation, before a big podcast interview, or before delivering a presentation to a large audience, I pause and write out how I want to feel at the end of the situation. I guarantee I do not write that I want to feel stress and extreme fear at the end of a presentation. Instead, I close my eyes, take what I wrote down, and I visualize feeling energized, motivated, and proud of the presentation delivered. Nine times out of ten, how I feel at the end of the situation or activity matched the intended feelings I visualized.

We can also use activities known to put us in an energized and happy state to rechannel fear, just as Robin used the stage and performance. Reflect on the activities that make up your days and support your life. Use them as your rechanneling outlets. If you feel those outlets do not exist right now, step out on an adventure to find them. Think of what lights you up and of hobbies that spark joy in your life; use them as your outlet to rechannel fear to positive energy.

Unfortunately, we lost Robin too early, and it saddens me to know that one of his greatest fears of losing control of his mind was one factor that cut his life short. The same mind that brought tears of laughter to many also brought tears of sadness when he passed. Whenever someone takes their own life, speculation as to why can run wild. I am not here to speculate, pass judgement, or draw any conclusions as to why we lost Robin.

What I hope you leave with is an inspiration to live your life as you, unapologetically. Life can be short, and it would be a shame for us not to fully experience the awesomeness that lives inside each of us. Although I wish Robin were still here today to spread joy, laughter, and energy into the world, I am grateful that he fully showed up during the years he was here.

Final Thought

Let the real you come out to play.

Who are the characters of my internal empire?

Jane Austen

Novelist whose works continue to be studied 200 years later

December 16, 1775 – July 18, 1817

QUICK BIO

- Considered one of the greatest writers in English history
- Most notable novels: *Sense and Sensibility* (1811), *Pride and Prejudice* (1813), *Mansfield Park* (1814), *Emma* (1815), *Northanger Abbey* (1817), *Persuasion* (1818)
- Gained global recognition over fifty years after her death
- Film and TV adaptations have been created based on *Emma, Mansfield Park, Pride and Prejudice, and Sense and Sensibility*
- *Pride and Prejudice* was sold to her publisher for £110 ($131 USD)

Behind the Question

Jane Austen is one of the most recognized authors in the world, yet throughout my journey of trying to understand who she was, I was left with more questions than answers. Over 200 years after she lived, how have her books never been out of print? Her books did not receive recognition outside her family and friends throughout her lifetime, and she was buried with minimal mention of her writing. However, her image has been proudly represented on British currency. Besides the Queen, she is the only woman to have received this honor.

Although it may be hard for us to accept, knowing how popular her work would become, Jane was content with her success. As literary critic Richard Blythe notes, "Literature, not the literary life, was always her intention." Her life events did not define her but more so defined her compelling personality—sassy, quick-witted, funny, and highly observant.

Jane's power of observation spawned the wildly relatable characters in her novels and inspired the prompts in this profile. There are elements of Jane in many of her characters, yet not any one represents all of who she was. Her sassiness, humor, and personality shine through various characters, contributing to her novels' power and relatability.

Let's return to the opening prompt and learn which characters shape our own lives. We can use the third person, which Jane is a master of doing through her writing, to unveil another perspective and view of our lives. We will do something different and have fun with the process. You get to be the Jane Austen of your life. You already have the characters of this novel; they comprise the person you are right now. As any classic novel, we have multiple characters fueling our stories. But often, we choose to identify with only a few of those characters resulting in the others being ignored.

I know I have a character fueling my internal empire who is happy, fun, and leaves people feeling energized after conversations. To the contrary, there is also a character who lives alone, is quiet, and has self-doubt, fear, and anxiety about his life. I would much rather hang out with the first character, but the reminder I received from Jane Austen's timeless works is that a great story has multiple personalities and characters. There are lessons to be learned from them all if we first identify who they are and what purposes they serve in our lives.

Turn your personality traits into characters of your movie with names and full bios to describe their personas. Take a moment to reflect on the story developing. There are no right or wrong storylines, characters, or plots. Be with those characters and see what comes up for you. You might like or dislike the story, but at least you know the story and understand the characters fueling the plot.

In many ways, Jane Austen is still a mystery to me, but she has left us with much to reflect on, whether to understand what makes a piece of work stand the test of time or to navigate self-discovery. The latter, which we cover here, is valuable in understanding the story we want to create for our lives irrespective of the era we live in.

What have I learned from my characters?

Jane Austen's most admired and memorable characters go through the most self-discovery. Take Elizabeth Bennet of *Pride and Prejudice*, who labelled her eventual husband (Fitzwilliam Darcy) as a person she would never spend her life with based on initial judgements around his wealth and power. As Dr. JoAnne Podis, professor of English at Ursuline College, notes, "Austen readers receive the message time and again that self-reflection in addition to self-awareness is an important part of realizing one's potential."

As the story unfolds, Elizabeth, day by day, releases her

initial judgments as she gets to know Fitzwilliam, and they eventually become a couple. I am not trying to spin a review on *Pride and Prejudice*, but there are valuable lessons in this one. Through the characters of *Pride and Prejudice*, I learned I quickly pass judgement on situations and that my relationship with money would be healthier if I were less impressed with it.

We are the authors of our own stories. We may not leave a 200-year-long legacy behind as Jane has through her work, but it's possible. Remember, during her lifetime she was not recognized as the literary legend we all know today. I am not suggesting you write a book, but you totally can if you feel motivated to do so. I am suggesting that you reflect on your life as if it were a classic piece of work that has the potential to stand the test of time. You deserve this! Thankfully, we have someone like Jane Austen to guide us.

Review the characters of yourself that you identified from the previous section of this profile and reflect on what they have taught you and where they are taking you. Now is the time for the plot twist: Make the changes supporting the person and story you want to live out. This reflective exercise does not take a tremendous amount of time to complete, but the results are high-value.

How will my story end?

We all share something in common—our stories will one day end. Like any good author, if we spend time on the details and crafting the events and characters to our story, we will have a higher probability for the ending we desire.

Our lives can quickly resemble a desk of scattered pages, but we can pull together a very compelling story through conscious reflection. Imagine if Jane Austen sat down and wrote without giving any thought to these critical elements. Sure, there would have been great material and learnings scattered throughout the pages, but they would have been just that, scattered pages without the glue of the binding holding the book together.

Reflect and understand what a life well-lived looks like for you. We have already prioritized time to understand the elements forming our story thus far: the characters, events, and ultimately the loose pages on our desk. Now it's time to pull it all together. This time can serve as an opportunity to adjust, edit, and narrow the focus of your story. Jane Austen scholars point to her limited subject, but incredible depth, as reason for her popularity and effectiveness.

Jane's narrow focus also makes me think of a point Chip Conley (see his profile for more on this topic) left me during our podcast together: "We spend the first half of our lives accumulating experiences, relationships, thoughts, and emotions. The second half of our lives is spent editing and removing what no longer supports our story." Regardless of where you may be in your life right now, you can never go wrong prioritizing time in reflection to understand what has made up your story to date, where it's naturally heading, and where you want it to end up.

Final Thought

Life is nothing but a story of events, characters, and emotions that shape the plot.

Who are the characters of my internal empire?

Why am I building this?

Scott Belsky

Fast Company's 100 Most Creative People in Business

QUICK BIO

- Executive, entrepreneur, author, and investor
- Cofounded Behance in 2006 and served as CEO until 2012
- Adobe's Chief Product Officer and Executive Vice President, Creative Cloud
- Obsessed with building products
- Author of the international best-selling books *Making Ideas Happen*, and *The Messy Middle* (one of my favorite books of all time)
- Investor in Pinterest, Uber, Sweetgreen, Carta, Cheddar, Flexport, Airtable, and Periscope (now part of Twitter) as well as several others in the early stages

---

Behind the Question

Scott's mind is a factory of creativity for new ideas, products, and services. He's a builder passionate about finding solutions for the people on the other side of his creations. However, Scott is also human and susceptible to personal passion overtaking his ideas—not seemingly a problem at first glance, until your solution does not align with what people need.

"Whenever I was building something out of the passion for my solution, as opposed to the empathy for the people suffering the problem, that's when things went wrong," says Belsky. In other words, creating while being empathetic to the real needs of the end consumer can lead to a much higher probability of success. This may sound obvious, but much easier said than done. There is a balance to be struck because most great ideas spark out of personal frustration with passion driving a desire to make the experience better.

My journaling app idea (KYO), or frustration with the digital options available at the time, sparked the personal passion required to go from idea to working on a solution. Passion is critical, but it can't be everything. This is where balance comes in. At one point, we need to shift from a sole personal passion to being empathetic to what others are suffering from. I am not a product expert, but there are many resources to help guide us in the right direction.

In the case of KYO, we waited too long to truly understand what our users needed and wanted, resulting in a business model not supported by our customers and the eventual closure of the app/business. Like many, we went too far solving for ourselves (with passion) while assuming our users would be on the same page. Sometimes this can work, but most times, as Scott mentions, you end up "30 degrees off or more from what the people need."

Please speak with your end consumers (earlier the better) to validate your solution in solving their problems. In writing out these words, it all seems overly simplistic and so obvious, leading my mind to think, "How did we wait so long to speak to our customers?" Everything always seems more evident in hindsight without the mental fog of emotions, decisions, and stress of surviving to the next day. However, I feel the opening prompt of this profile, "Why am I building this?" would have been incredibly helpful to consistently reflect on throughout my journey of building KYO.

The prompt serves two purposes:
1. Motivator to keep pushing through
2. Reminder to be empathetic to the problem you are solving for your end users

I will pause my own mental narrative right now, which is making me feel like I should have known better, and cut myself some slack because I know I was in a phase of business that is incredibly challenging and often not discussed. Scott has written extensively about this phase of business and has labelled it "the messy middle."

How do I navigate the messy middle?

If you are following the sequence of this profile, then the *why* of what you are building is becoming clear, and by default the *what* should be following the same path. But, the *what* of a product or services usually takes more experimentation and iteration. At this point, you have left the stage of excitement for the novelty of the new idea where everyone around you lights up about the new project you're working on. Now, you have to execute, work extremely hard, and often feel like your head is bobbing in and out of the water to catch another breath and stay afloat. It's hard, really hard, and probably why we don't hear about this stage of the journey as often. This is the *messy middle.*

The messy middle is critical to building businesses, products, services, and your life. As Scott Belsky describes in his book *The Messy Middle,* "While difficult to withstand and tempting to rush, the middle contains all the discoveries that build your capacity. The middle is messy, but it yields the unexpected bounty that makes all the difference." Cheers to that! Let's embrace the mess for the bounty it can deliver, but leverage mental fitness practices to not only survive but thrive in the messy middle.

Like most things in life, a rock-solid mind is paramount. The middle of the journey will test every part of your existence and lead you into questioning whether it will ever work out or if you will ever be able to have a salary to support yourself and about a million other combinations of these questions. Scott has a great solution to pause and reframe the internal narratives: mental gymnastics. Mental gymnastics is mind hacks for you and your team to stay motivated during the messy middle.

Scott uses concepts like office billboards to consistently trigger his team's subconscious minds in a positive way. As an example from his days at Behance, they had an office billboard stating, "Maybe one day we will no longer be a mistake," in reference to Google autocorrecting *Behance,* a made-up word, to *enhance* each time someone was searching for their company. It was one simple line on the wall, but it lightened the team's mood and pressure as they built the company, which went on to be acquired by Adobe.

Think of the phrases, quotes, and reflections that you or your team could benefit from. Take a pause from reading this profile, go find them, and put them in a place where they will be seen often. I personally use *mental* billboards. My iPhone lock screen wallpaper currently has a line from the best-selling author of *The 5 AM Club,* Robin Sharma that reads, "Dedication and discipline beat brilliance and giftedness every day of the week." According to my screen time report, I pick up my phone and prime my mind with this mantra an average of forty-nine times per day.

Another favorite concept of Scott's is intentionally narrating progress: "It's the progress that you narrate that is the motivator of future progress." We often default to celebrating only the big wins, but when you're in the thick of creating a business, the big wins can take years. They are usually the combination of many micro wins over time, or in other words, progress. All progress is vital. Highlight, share, and celebrate your progress! I'm not only talking about businesses and products. It's equally important to celebrate your personal progress. If you got up five minutes earlier today to work on your mental fitness—celebrate and be proud! Five minutes today leads to another five minutes tomorrow and can progress to hours, days, and years over time.

Now is the time to pause and think. It is not my intention to provide a prescriptive set of hacks to navigate your mind, but to help you come to those reflections on your own. You are much more likely to execute and stick with them if they come from you and support your circumstances. Have fun with the process and try different hacks, but make sure you are always seeking feedback from your team and from yourself. As Scott says, "Feedback is the alternative form of compensation."

Successfully being able to mentally navigate the middle of the journey provides the opportunity to reach the end—an acquisition of your product, a significant injection of capital, an initial public offering (IPO), a profitable business, happy customers, a motivated team, or a fulfilled life. Only you know the end goal, and it might change over time. But one thing is for sure, you will not reach the end without going through the middle.

Should I stop or keep going?

This is one of the most important, yet scariest, questions any founder can ask themselves. I speak from experience, having asked myself this very question and also being terrified by the answer. Scott has a simple, yet rugged, framing to the question: "Do you have as much, if not more, conviction in the end state than you had in the beginning, or do you have less?" The significance of the framing is critical. In the beginning, it's all rainbows and butterflies, pure excitement about the potential that lies ahead. Then reality sets in. We see the complexities, the challenges, the real picture required to bring our initial idea to light. We enter the messy middle. From this place, if your conviction is firm or has increased, keep going. If that's not the case, it's okay to be honest with yourself.

In the end, my answer was no, and I had to stop. I did not have the same level of conviction as I had when I first shared KYO's initial concept. Somewhere along the way, as I gathered more information and insight, I lost the conviction required to navigate the messy middle and come out on the other side. Even though at the time it felt horrible and like the world was exploding around me, this was the best decision I could have made for myself. It was extremely painful, but also lifted a substantial mental weight from my body that allowed me to now focus on the next phase of my journey. Part of this journey includes you and this book, which could not make me any happier.

Always be honest with yourself. You and the people around you deserve it.

Final Thought

To be honest with others, we first have to be honest with ourselves.

How can I be the most curious person in the room?

Chip Conley
Rebel hospitality entrepreneur

QUICK BIO

- At age twenty-six he founded Joie de Vivre Hospitality (JdV), transforming an inner-city motel into the second largest boutique hotel brand in America
- Sold JdV after running it as CEO for twenty-four years
- Awarded Most Innovative CEO by the *San Francisco Business Times* and hospitality's highest honor, the Pioneer Award
- *New York Times* best-selling author
- Authored five books covering the intersection of psychology and business
- The founders of Airbnb asked him to help transform their promising start-up into the world's leading hospitality brand
- Served as Airbnb's Head of Global Hospitality and Strategy for four years and today acts as the company's Strategic Advisor for Hospitality and Leadership

Behind the Question

I asked Chip the same question I ask each guest on the *Behind The Human Podcast:* "Who are you?" Chip answered, "I'm a curious white boy." I immediately knew I was in for a fantastic interview. Chip is a fifty-nine-year-old curiosity master attacking each stage of his life with powerful, reflective questions. He explained how life typically starts with the deeper "why and what if" questions, but quickly shifts to more shallow, optimizing questions like "what and how."

We default down this line of questioning as we get older because we seek to be more efficient and productive. No fault of our own; society is not set up to reward the time required to reflect on why and what questions. Many have discovered, including Chip, at some point in midlife we end up coming back to more thought-provoking questions. Many lose sight of who they are or have never found that person in the first place.

Why wait for that traumatic life roadblock or burn out to start asking these questions again? In Chip's words, "These questions lead to the breadcrumbs of life," and when we see and follow them, great opportunities start showing up. We can do this by organizing our lives to include time and place for reflection. Considering you are reading through these pages, you took the first step. However, the next and most critical step is interacting with the knowledge and understanding if you are being dominated by low-impact questions or high-quality and life-shaping prompts.

It may seem like I've gone off on a tangent from how to be the most curious person in the room, but to be that person, you have to exercise your curiosity muscles first. What better place to start than with yourself? Over time, your curiosity will naturally develop, and you will also notice the space increasing between your thoughts and reactions, essentially giving you a massive advantage through a microsecond pause that many do not know exists or how to access. That pause, combined with your heightened sense of curiosity, can lead to authentic and powerful questions, comments, observations, and revelations.

Building in weekly mental fitness practices will exercise these mental muscles, or as Chip says, "Meditation slows my mind down, and exercise takes me out of my mind." These are the exercises that work for Chip, but for you they might be different. Explore the activities you already know make you feel great. Those activities might include taking a walk in the forest, doing yoga, or going for a long drive. Find what feels right for you and supports consistent mental fitness in your routine.

Am I truly present?

There is a beautiful byproduct that comes with being the most curious person in the room. It's something hard to measure, but priceless in value. Chip defines this byproduct as karmic capitalism: giving your complete presence to people who in turn benefit us in ways we cannot imagine.

The opposite of presence is absence, and we know how absence makes us feel. Think of the one who is continually looking over your shoulder for the next subject, or that person who is more interested in the alerts firing off on their phone or smartwatch than the person in front of them. These behaviors quickly make us feel like we are not worthy of their time. Unfortunately, given the explosive growth of 24-hour connectivity and content, these behaviors have started to be accepted as normal. Fortunately, if we decide to take Chip's advice, shifting from absence to presence will easily allow us to stand out from the crowd.

You can feel when a person is truly with you. They listen, empathize, and are genuinely curious. Use curiosity as your tool to unlock persistent presence. Set yourself up for success. Put away devices, turn off notifications, and eliminate distractions you know can easily pull you away from being present. This includes virtual meetings where it's even easier to be distracted as we think we can fool the people on the other side.

Try the following as an experiment. For one week, start the morning with this intention: I will be fully present today in all communications with other people. When in a conversation, work on training your curiosity muscles. Think of something you'd love to know about that person and ask them about it. Listen to the words coming out of their mouth and pay attention to their facial expressions as they answer. At the end of each day, journal on one question: How was I curious today? In a few short minutes of reflection, we can see our progress, or lack thereof, leaving us with valuable information to make any necessary adjustments.

If you want to be the most curious person in the room or the best at anything, it will always come down to daily habits and systems put in place to support your goals. Take the time to understand if your habits, practices, and systems are fuelling your goals and desires or having the opposite effect, pushing you further away from achieving the outcomes you want.

Who are my modern elders?

Let me first provide context behind the term "modern elder." It started when Chip Conley received a call from Brian Chesky, one of the young founders of Airbnb, asking him to help grow their start-up into a global hospitality giant. He was fifty-two at the time and referred to by the team as the elder, a term he hated. Sure he was much older than most of the employees at Airbnb, but he didn't feel older and he also had decades of experience and knowledge to offer. The word "elder," particularly in North America, carries a connotation of being old and on the way out from life, not at all how Chip would define himself.

Chip redefined his label from elder to modern elder, someone as curious as they are wise. He has since gone on to write *Wisdom at Work: The Making of a Modern Elder* and to open up the first Modern Elder Academy, a school dedicated to helping people navigate midlife.

Finding those in our lives who are as curious as they are wise is a definitive way to accelerate the training of our curiosity muscles while propelling our lives forward. Modern elders come preloaded with rich and powerful reflective questions, making perfect mentors.

Chip defines the best mentors as "...not the ones who offer answers to you, they are the people who train you to think differently and ask different questions of yourself." These questions are derived from decades of wisdom and which surface at the most appropriate times in our lives. Those times where we might feel lost or are struggling to see a clear path forward, our modern elders can help. The chances are high that they have experienced something similar in the past and can provide perspective, guidance, and the questions required to unlock the answers we seek.

Think of the modern elders in your life or who you want in your life. List these people on a sheet of paper. Set the intention to connect with them and think of where you need the most guidance right now. Before reaching out to your modern elder, write in detail about the situation in which you seek advice. Then narrow these details down to one straightforward question or sentence. Our modern elders often graciously want to help, but we should also respect their time and wisdom by showing up prepared.

There are also hidden benefits when going through a preparatory practice as described above. You might very well come out with the answers you seek on your own by breaking down and explaining the situation. The answers to our questions often surface when we take time to extract the details from our minds and physically see them written out on a fresh piece of paper.

How can I cultivate inner curiosity?

Do you know that nagging pain that shows up in our shoulders or around our neck when we go full throttle in life? This pain is what Chip refers to as "the psychic toll" of how we live our lives each day. It's a physical pain manifesting from the consistent mental tension that we typically overlook until physical symptoms arise. However, if we were to slow down and connect with our body, we would catch that tension before it becomes a more significant issue. Chip has a set of questions to slow down and connect with his body:

- How do I feel this week?
- How fresh and engaged do I feel?

These prompts help us slow down and uncover signs of tension so we can course-correct on the spot before physical symptoms surface. The more we intentionally reflect on how we feel, the easier it becomes to recognize when things start to slip. We will no longer be hitting catastrophic walls *forcing* change; instead, we can make micro-adjustments along the way led by our curiosity.

One of the most rewarding outcomes of putting our internal curiosity to work is defining who we are or who we want to become. The answers to these questions often shift throughout a lifetime. Chip suggests we have a close friend ask us "Who am I?" a minimum of five times in a row to get to the bottom of the answer. When we have clarity in who we are or who we are striving to be, the next steps, decisions, and path forward also become apparent.

Final Thought

The most curious person in the room is also the most present.

How can I be the most curious person in the room?

Who am I?

Nikki Sharp

Wellness-obsessed international model, entrepreneur, and author

QUICK BIO

- Created the #1 rated *5-Day Detox* app
- Best-selling author of *The 5-Day Real Food Detox* and *Meal Prep Your Way to Weight Loss: 28 Days to a Fitter, Healthier You*
- Dedicated to making health sexy via the mind, body, and soul
- Featured in *Forbes, Huffington Post, Shape, Women's Health*, and *Vogue*

Behind the Question

The most powerful and life-shaping narrative comes after two simple words: I am. What we say after these two words defines the person we are. Whether we like, respect, or believe in that person does not matter. Our words result from what we think and what we think shapes who we become. What's amazing about this concept is that we can change our words at any point. It's precisely what Nikki decided to do, and it changed her life for the better.

Nikki started modeling at the age of sixteen. She appeared on the cover of magazines and was quickly developing a prosperous and exciting career as an internationally recognized model. "I am a model," is how Nikki defined herself at that time. For many, this would be a dream, and it was for Nikki as well, but the label also came with another set of consequences she did not envision nor realize was normal. She was hospitalized with stomach issues, took sedatives to sleep, medicated herself for skin and eating disorders, all while having every part of her body measured and scrutinized. It's not the life she envisioned for herself. Enough was enough. She decided to respect her body and herself.

Nikki shifted her life by focusing on the narrative following those two critical words "I am." Knowing she was "happiest when helping others," she decided to refocus her life to serve. She reflected on who she wanted to be and how she wanted to show up daily, realizing that through her healing journey she could help millions of people worldwide. She has done just that through her books, speaking, programs, and now modelling again, but through a different perspective. It's through the confidence of knowing who she is, what she stands for, and serving others by lifting them up so they thrive in their own lives.

Think of how you define yourself at this very moment. At the bottom of this page, in the margin, complete the sentence "I am..." without thinking about it. Let whatever words come out of your mind surface on the page. Do not judge or criticize what comes out. Be with who you are right now in this moment. There are no right or wrong answers, only data and insight.

Now that you consciously know how you define yourself, decide whether this is the person you want to be or not. Write out these one-liner statements for the areas in your life most important to you. Understand how you show up or want to show up as a coworker, friend, parent, sibling, spouse, and yourself. If you want to go ever deeper around character reflection, flip to Jane Austen's profile. Celebrate the areas of your life where you are showing up as the person you want to be. Write a congratulatory statement like, "Yes, I did that. I put in the work to become...," right beside the "I am" statement and feel the self-love. You deserve it!

For the areas you know there is a disconnect, please don't pretend you don't know and don't attempt to justify the words you wrote. This is a no-judgement exercise sticking to the facts. Write down who you want to be. Stay with "I am" because this will also serve as an intention for you, priming your mind to seek elements and actions that will get you to the person you are striving to be.

Remember to be kind to yourself. All change is uncomfortable at the start, messy in the middle, but beautiful at the end. Start small, and reflect on the daily actions required for the shift you desire. Take a look at what you have scheduled each day, and note what you do during unscheduled or free time. Where you dedicate your time and effort is either matching who you want to be or pushing you further from that person. Write down the actions or corrections required, and scan them each morning to keep them in your subconscious while also tracking your progress. Most importantly, when you have reached your milestones, celebrate the wins!

As Nikki was recalibrating her relationship with nutrition and respect for her body, she completely changed her association with exercising and the gym. Instead of using the gym as a punishment for binge eating, she reversed the relationship making the gym a reward for eating clean and healthy. This helped change her eating behaviors and rewarded her with something she liked doing, a perfect example of a mindset shift leading to actionable change and ultimately forming the person Nikki was striving to become.

What are my happiness triggers?

Nikki used exercise, specifically running, as a tool throughout her transformative journey to shift, prime, and allow her mind to thrive. It's a tool that many, including myself, leverage as a way to shift our minds into a happy state. Exercise in general can serve this purpose for many, but as Nikki often states, "You have to find something you love doing. If you do something you hate, you will never see the results you want. Do something you love and the results will come."

Understanding our happiness triggers is vital when working through uncomfortable change and is a superpower that can be used daily. It's a way to keep our minds in a state of motivation and creation. Let's intentionally seek and understand what lights us up, so we, too, can have the power of turning on happiness at any moment.

Nikki uses a three-list approach to do this. Take out a blank sheet of paper and divide it into three sections. In the first section, list everything you are certain makes you feel happy. For example, activities like exercising, spending time with close friends, journaling, taking a walk, or doing a round of breathwork are some of my happiness triggers. There is no secret recipe I can prescribe. We are all different, and your list has to resonate with you. A good measure to understand what should be on the list is by identifying the things that put a smile on your face or leave you feeling motivated.

Use the second section to list your typical day. Include everything you do on an average day. I mean everything, from the moment your eyes open in the morning to the time they close at night.

Now for the moment of truth. Using the third section, map out the disconnects from your happiness list and what you actually do daily. Are your days filled with the things that make you happy or something else? I'm not suggesting that we have to embark on a 24-hour happiness fest, but if the items on list one (what makes you happy) are not consistently showing up in our lives, how can we expect to feel great?

I recently moved outside of Toronto to a smaller and more active outdoor-centric community. I love being in nature: mountain biking, snowboarding (this is new and I'm loving it!), hiking, and walking in silence. Any one of these activities can shift my mind from a self-destructive internal narrative to a positive, motivated, and often flow state of mind.

When I did my calendar audit, though, these activities were only showing up on the weekends. If I know they put me in a positive and creative state of mind, should they not be showing up during the week as well? The answer is yes, but I, like many, are programmed to think these types of activities during the week will reduce my productivity. I'm not suggesting you start blowing off meetings to go snowboarding in the middle of the day, but to find a balance.

After I eat lunch, I try to take a short walk, even if only ten minutes, to move my body and clear my mind in order to rock the afternoon. On my writing days, I schedule in something more intense like a bike ride or a couple snowboard runs to put me in a flow state which carries over to my writing.

As soon as ski season starts, *New York Times* best-selling author and Flow Research expert, Steven Kotler, schedules time on the hill. The flow states triggered by skiing directly affect the quality of his work, and the boost in creativity has been shown to last up to three days after the flow state. If you want to go deeper on flow states, I highly recommend Steven's book, *The Art of Impossible* and my interview with him on *Behind The Human* podcast (Episode #154).

The mental magic shows up when we can consistently loop in items that light us up in our daily routines. What's even better, they can be the smallest acts yet yield the biggest returns. Taking a ten-minute walk before jumping into your next task, or sending a friend a text expressing how much they mean to you, only takes seconds but can leave them *and* you feeling great all day.

Creating a happiness list and being armed with that self-knowledge at a moment's notice is a game-changer when faced with unexpected stress, uncertainty, and fear. We can default to any item on our list to break the internal narrative that is driving unwanted emotions and holding us back from being the person we want to be.

As loaded as a question like "Who am I?" can appear to be at first glance, breaking the prompt down into one-liner "I am" statements and intentionally directing your energy and actions to support them can go a long way. Getting clear on who we are or who we want to be does not have to be complicated or have to soak up a tremendous amount of time, yet the results can completely change your life.

Final Thought

Where and how you invest your energy dictates who you will become.

What do I want to do before I die?

Ben Nemtin

Living out his bucket list

QUICK BIO

- Happy kid, until debilitating depression hit and everything changed
- Lost his academic scholarship, his dream of making the U-19 rugby team, and he dropped out of college
- Made a bucket list with friends that changed his life (and others' lives)
- #1 *New York Times* best-selling author of *What Do You Want To Do Before You Die*?
- Star of the MTV show *The Buried Life*
- Played basketball with President Obama, made it on *Oprah*, and helped others live out their bucket lists

---

Behind the Question

This one question has made the impossible possible for millions of people around the world. For Ben, playing basketball with President Obama at the White House, appearing on *Oprah*, and having a beer with Prince Harry are just a few examples of what is possible when you pause to make a bucket list and then live it out. As Ben has stated in many of his keynote presentations around the world, "The single biggest regret people have at the end of their [lives] is not what they did but what they didn't do."

After surveying hundreds of participants through six studies, psychologist and Cornell University graduate, Thomas Gilovich, concluded that 76% of participants said their single biggest regret in life was not fulfilling their ideal self. When I first heard this statistic from Ben, it hit home and made me wonder: Where am I playing it safe in life? Where am I holding back? What would I regret if today was my last day? I would regret not writing this book. I would regret not giving it my all and also regret not being present to enjoy the journey and process required to get this book in your hands.

Here's where you stop reading. Pick up a pen, and in the margin of the page, list three things you want to do before you die. We will come back to this list soon.

What dreams am I burying?

We all have dreams, but something often holds us back from pursuing those dreams: fear. With Ben's mentality, the good news is we can move past our fears and live out our bucket lists and surround ourselves with people who support the list. As Ben witnessed, "All of these things we were convinced were impossible...have happened." How do we make the impossible possible?

I'll never forget the magic Ben was able to create in a room filled with curious people. He arrived in Toronto and delivered a live presentation for Lululemon on the topic of creating and living out your bucket list. I remember thinking, "What can we possibly talk about for an hour related to creating a list?" I naively made the assumption that making a list is all it takes. Wow, was I wrong. Sure, we can make our bucket list, but making a list and checking things off that list are two different things.

All participants in the room took five minutes to make their list and then turned to a stranger to share their top items. It seems like a small action, but something changes when others are brought into the equation. Now, it feels real. Even though I did not know the person beside me, I immediately felt a sense of accountability, not necessarily toward that person but to myself since they now knew what was on my list.

I started to see why Ben was speaking all around the world about his process, and it was only about to get better. People in the room began sharing with the other fifty participants the number one thing they wanted to do before they died. Quickly, the entire room got involved, "I can help with that! I know someone who can make that happen!" It was remarkable to witness what were seemingly impossible dreams just minutes ago working their way to becoming realities. This is possible for you right now!

- What do I want to do before I die?
- Who are the people in my circle who can help me live out my list (friends, family, coworkers, my social network connections, etc.?)
- Who can I help to live out their dreams?

Ben has helped countless people identify and realize their dreams, and here's how we can help Ben! Message him on social media if you can help with any remaining items left on his list:

- Be on the cover of *Rolling Stone* (#15)
- Tell a judge: "You want the truth? You can't handle the truth!" (#26)
- Recreate *The Notebook* scene with Rachel McAdams (#55)

- Pay off our parents' mortgages (#87)
- Experience zero gravity (#89)
- Host *Saturday Night Live* (#99)
- Go to space (#100)

Who knows about my list?

Something powerful happens when you set intentions for what you want in your life and share it with others. People, situations, and opportunities start showing up to fulfill these intentions. Ben and his group of friends witnessed the power of the ripple effect from the beginning. After sharing his list with friends, he later commented, "Look at this inbox. Hundreds of emails have rolled in with people wanting to help."

The most beautiful part of the ripple effect is how lives will change in ways we cannot even begin to imagine. For example, when the guys from The Buried Life noticed the trending hashtag #HandForTorri (Thanks, Chris Messina for the #!), they sourced the best bionic arm on the market and surprised her at the Invisible Children Fourth Estate Summit. At nineteen years old, it was the first time she was able to hug her father.

The most critical point is that people can't help if they don't know what to help with. We first need to release any fear, judgement, or worry of what others (and ourselves) will think of our list. Secondly, actively share the list to capitalize on the power of the ripple effect.

How can I rechannel stress, anxiety, and fear?

Delivering keynotes in front of tens of thousands of people about how to unlock your mind and achieve your wildest dreams was the last thing Ben Nemtin was thinking about when he was debilitated by his own anxiety. Before his friends pulled him out of this spiralling loop, he got to the point where he could no longer make decisions for himself. His life was quickly unravelling. He had an academic scholarship to a top-tier school and had just made the U-19 Canadian rugby team. But it all stopped. He no longer attended classes or practices or anything that required him to leave the house.

I share Ben's experiences with anxiety and depression because he knows how it feels to be held back by his mind. However, now he knows how to reduce stress, worry, and fear from any situation. Ben uses the emotions that once held him back as a sign or a trigger to go all in with the situation in front of him. For example, when he was asked to give a commencement speech for the University of Utah, the first thought that came to mind was he did not want to do it. His internal narrative started to fire: How many people would be in the crowd? Will my family see this speech? Am I the right person to send all these graduates off into the world? Ben recognized his mental chatter, and instead of closing down, he flipped the script and took the fear as a sign that he had to deliver the speech.

Everything in his body was firing—fear, nerves, and self-doubt flooding his mind and body. The difference now versus when he was debilitated by these same feelings in the past was his mindset. He knew he could grow exponentially by rechanneling these feelings to fuel his experience and prepare him for the ones to come. In a way, he seeks this discomfort because he can press fast-forward on his growth.

At this point, I'm sure you're thinking, "Sure sounds easy, but in reality, how do I do this?" It's a logical thought, and here are a couple critical factors I've learned from Ben supporting his mindset. He surrounds himself with great, motivating, and inspiring people to continually fuel and prime his mind. But, what if you're not friends with Richard Branson or Oprah? Thankfully due to books, podcasts, and everything available online, we all have incredible people of the highest caliber at our fingertips.

When top-level humans consistently surround you, you naturally absorb their wisdom and thinking. It's like having the best coaches in the world to handle any situation available to you at all times. Think about it. If you consume a podcast every day with content that primes your mind at elite levels, your mind will start trending to this very same place.

Another mental hack from Ben is something I like to call "experience stacking." Taking the feelings and experiences from past situations and leveraging them to reframe any fear or worry in the present moment. Let me explain by going back to Ben's commencement speech. His self-talk was, "Well, it can't be any worse than being arrested for streaking in front of 10,000 people (#50 on his bucket list)." These experiences continue to compound, and over time we release the initial fears that in the past would have held us back.

Time to make another list, one you can always turn to when faced with situations that spark fear. List every situation you can remember that made you feel scared, nervous, or uncomfortable, but that you conquered. First of all, celebrate this; it's awesome! We quickly forget these moments, but they are the exact situations you want to "experience stack" to rechannel the emotions holding you back from your next opportunity. Go for it, live life to the max, and enjoy the ride!

Final Thought

What you think is impossible today, can be a reality tomorrow.

How can I be clearer in fewer words?

Mikael Cho

Cofounder of the most used image asset library ever (Unsplash)

QUICK BIO

- Created the first version of Unsplash (acquired by Getty Images) in three hours with $38 and a Tumblr blog
- Built an automated creative agency that booked more work than the top creative agencies in the world
- Created the world's first fully-crowdsourced open book (*The Unsplash Book*)
- Created the #1 ranked (by *Forbes*) most beautiful coworking spaces in the world (Crew Collective)
- Featured writer in *Inc.*, *TED*, and *ABC News*

———

Behind the Question

There are a handful of people in present-day life who immediately stop me in my tracks and spark reflection simply through a few powerful words. Cal Fussman, James Clear, Seth Godin (hope to profile one day), and Mikael Cho are those people. At any point, while reading this profile, if you feel inspired to do so, take a pause and go directly to @mikaelcho on Twitter and explore his reflections on business and life. You will not be disappointed.

Straight from Mikael's feed:

"Write simple. Extra words are fear."

"Most problems come from conflicting priorities. Focus removes conflict."

"If you're having trouble building good habits, try breaking the bad ones instead."

"You're more likely to fail by doing too much too soon than doing too little too long."

One of Mikael's tweets hits home when I read, "The best antidote for building a product no one wants is to build something you want." KYO started from this exact philosophy. After years of using digital journals I was always left frustrated that there were no options to seamlessly interact and reflect on powerful prompts. As it turned out, I was not the only one, given the wildly fast uptake of the app and hundreds of thousands of people who were using KYO.

As you have gathered by now, I flip most things into questions, so when I consume reflections from someone like Mikael, the same process applies. For example, here are Mikael's tweets into questions I've reflected on:

"Write simple. Extra words are fear." Where
in my life am I using extra words?

*"Most problems come from conflicting priorities. Focus
removes conflict."* Do I have conflicting priorities?

*"If you're having trouble building good hab-
its, try breaking the bad ones instead."* What's one
bad habit I can work on eliminating today?

*"You're more likely to fail by doing too much too soon than
doing too little too long."* Where am I doing too much?

Any piece of content can be combined with intentional re-flection. I believe the combination of these two practices (learning + reflection) is the fastest and most efficient path to expanding possibility and opportunity.

Quality pieces of content, like Mikael's Twitter reflections, force us to pause, tilting our head and eyes upwards in thought from what we just read. This is good, but then journaling on what you consumed and how it links to your life today is even better. Your mind is primed, in a creative state, and is ready to surface reflections, ideas, or insights to guide you. Most people don't do this. They skim through content in search of the next piece of content without ever pausing and implementing the learning in their lives.

Mikael trains his mind daily with one of the most unique journaling practices I have seen to date. It is an approach that can help us be clearer, precise, and focused on shipping the best projects. Let's call this practice Getting Clear: 280 Twitter-character-limits clear.

What are my 280 characters?

Over the years, I have seen many people use platforms like Instagram and Facebook to share longer streams of thought, what I call public journaling, often intended to be consumed and then dialogued in the comments. Mikael has a different objective when using Twitter to write, one that I believe trains his mind to think at an elite level. Mikael shared, "I used to write to be read; now I write to understand." Take a minute, reread that, and let it sink in. I had one of those push-your-chair-back-in-thought moments to let that line fully land.

I started writing this book thinking I was organizing a 60,000 piece jigsaw puzzle by similar shapes and colors. However, the real magic and the most mentally-stimulating aspect of the entire journey has been figuring out how those pieces fit together. I was under the illusion that one piece had to belong in a certain place, but in fact it ended up in the complete opposite corner. To use Mikael's thinking, this is writing to understand. The more I write, the more I understand and the clearer the puzzle becomes. The next move, words, decisions, and actions surface out of putting in the work and practice.

Here's how Mikael does it: Many of the Twitter reflections we see in his feed originate during early morning walks, a time when life and the day are still quiet. A thought will surface, he'll capture it (at the time using his phone), and then let that thought sit. We can apply this method to many aspects of life: the spark of a new idea, a business model pivot, or a thought we want to express to the world. Let these ideas and thoughts sit. Give them space to breathe, and as Mikael does, come back to them the next morning to mold the concept or craft it further.

When time passes, the noise and bright, shiny objects surrounding our thoughts dissipate, leaving us with something more pure and meaningful. Think about your 280 characters. Where could you use this level of clarity in your life right now? Even if you have no intent on posting to Twitter, try out the 280 character limit journaling practice for the next week. Have fun with it, explore what's possible, and enjoy the opportunity that will come along with focusing your thoughts and ideas.

Final Thought

Less is often more.

How can I be clearer in fewer words?

What is my art reflecting?

Pablo Picasso

Spanish painter who pioneered the Cubism art movement

October 25, 1881 – April 8, 1973

QUICK BIO

- Considered one of the most influential artists of the 20th century
- Spanish-born artist who spent most of working artist career in France
- Created more than 50,000 works
- Along with George Braque, Picasso is credited with creating Cubism, a controversial style represented by construed geometric shapes
- Learned art from his father
- Wrote poems, plays, designed costumes and sets for ballets

_____

Behind the Question

My immediate reaction to concluding the research on Picasso is to run to the nearest museum and take in Picasso's art through an entirely different lens. In fact, I did just that (virtually) through the Picasso Museum Barcelona, a museum I once visited in person during a much different time in my life. It was a period that makes me think of something Picasso once said, "I do not seek. I find." When I physically visited the museum in Barcelona, I was in a seeking phase of my life. I was seeking the perfect job, the validation, the titles, and the next best thing. I'm not holding judgement toward myself, but merely observing the place my mind was during that visit. I was more focused on making my way through the entire museum to see every piece of art, versus now, where I strive to experience even just one piece of his art with presence and curiosity.

Now, I see the details and am finding my place in this world. I am creating the life that feels most right for me. Through Picasso's wisdom and story, I feel confident and comforted knowing that he, too, endlessly reinvented himself while switching between styles of art throughout his life.

When looking at Picasso's body of work, wildly different styles appear. These styles represent the thoughts and emotions running through his mind during a given period. Take Picasso's Blue Period, for example, where we often see his subjects looking down with somber expressions and themes like blindness and poverty. Historians attribute this phase of Picasso's work to depression he was experiencing from the suicide of a close friend. Then, the dominant color shifted from blue to rose and other cheerful colors. It has been suggested that a new romantic relationship with Fernande Olivier was the reason for this style change.

In both periods of Picasso's life, some of his most famous paintings show up. Take *The Old Guitarist* from his blue period and *Garçon à la Pipe* (*Boy With a Pipe*) from the rose period. With a quick Google search you will see the differences in color, expression, and emotion.

> *"Colors, like features, follow the changes of the emotions."* —*Pablo Picasso*

My point being, Picasso's life, like ours, consists of different stages. Given, we can recognize these periods in his legendary work. We, too, can leverage this creative expression to see our own lives through a different lens, to see how our "styles" have evolved over the years and how they contribute to our body of work—our life.

What color period am I in right now?

Let's open up the creative side of our minds, slow down, and be our own Picasso. Draw out the years of your life in five- or ten-year segments and attach a color to each. If this time frame does not feel right to you, pick another, but having a segment will make the reflection easier. Think about why you associated the colors to those stages of your life and understand the prominent emotions behind them. Don't rush the process. Take the time to write all the details you can recall. If you feel comfortable doing so, share your reflections with a long-time friend who was with you throughout these periods and ask what colors they select for you.

When going through this exercise, I noticed my colors shifted as I moved from my childhood into my mid-thirties. As an adult, I spent much time in the reds: pushing, grinding, and stressing. After doing the inner work, lighter, more playful colors emerge. When we push or repel, we are met with equal resistance. Through many mental fitness practices in this book, I have learned, and continue to learn, how to release the resistance. I am now more driven, aligned, and ready to jump at opportunities.

There are no right or wrong answers or colors. The point is not to cast judgement on the different phases of your life, but to gather insight. Then, we must decide whether we want to act upon the insights or not. As Picasso once said, "The purpose of art is washing the dust of daily life off our souls." Let's see what surfaces when we wash the dust off our art and the experiences that make up our lives.

What am I not seeing?

There are two ways we typically experience art. We can walk through the Picasso Museum Barcelona, quickly glancing at Picasso's work; or we can stop, look, and feel (emotionally) the art, allowing it to pique our curiosity. I opened the profile with a personal example describing my first experience with Picasso's work and linked this to a period in my life when I was seeking. The difference from then to now is the "stop, look, feel, and be curious" aspect, which can also translate to other aspects of life.

Imagine you looked at a project, challenge, or business idea through the same curious eyes you would a Picasso painting. What do you see, or what are you not seeing? Look at the detail, and think of the experiences stacked together forming your interpretation of the situation. Often, the first glance is just that, a first glance and not always the full story. Take Picasso's iconic painting *The Old Guitarist,* which upon further research and X-rays reveal a ghostly image of a woman painted underneath. The more we look, the more we see and understand. Picasso says it best: "The hidden harmony is better than the obvious." Let's explore our hidden harmonies and see what stories they tell.

The greatest gift art has given me is the ability to slow down and notice the detail. I believe that experiencing art trains our mental muscles to be more curious and allows us to see more connections and associations than the untrained mind. Contemplate where you can include more art in your life. Use it as one of your mental training exercises, but also for the stillness it brings. Respect the artist on the other side, who also happens to be you, and be present with their work while allowing your mind to focus on one thing—the art before your eyes.

What is unnecessary?

We have reflected upon our lives to review and understand the periods making up the person we are. We have also slowed down to notice the detail and what we may be missing below the surface. Now, it is time to eliminate the unnecessary and be our truest selves. Picasso says, "Art is the elimination of the unnecessary." Let's paint the picture of where we are heading by thinking of the story we want to tell. Picasso's masterpieces were created from the interpretations he made of other art and his experiences of the time. The same can be done with our lives.

Take time to slow down, eliminate distractions and judgement from others (or yourself), and be clear in what you want on your canvas of life. As we have seen with *The Old Guitarist*, it can take many iterations and require us to paint over previous work to reach the final result we are ready to present to the world. It's through this experimentation and discovery that we find the person we want to be, not someone else, but the real you.

This line by Picasso summarizes the point and landed strongly with me: "When I was a child, my mother said to me,

'If you become a soldier, you'll be a general. If you become a monk, you'll end up as the Pope.' Instead, I became a painter and wound up as Picasso."

Final Thought

Legacy is created from our full body of work, not individual phases of our lives.

What expectations am I holding in my relationships?

Melissa Ambrosini

Author of top-rated self-esteem books & #1 podcast host

QUICK BIO

- Inspires others to reclaim their power, step into their truth, live with intention, and move in the direction of their dreams
- Believes that love is sexy, health is liberating, and wealth isn't a dirty word
- Love, sex, and relationship guide for the modern woman
- Best-selling author of *Mastering Your Mean Girl*, *Open Wide*, *Comparisonitis*, and the Audible original *PurposeFULL*
- Host of the top-rated podcast *The Melissa Ambrosini Show*

Behind the Question

When I think of Melissa Ambrosini, warm glowing energy passes through my mind leaving me with a grand smile. She is a gift to this planet, choosing to live life through love instead of fear and open instead of closed. Throughout my interviews with her, she was dropping prompts like, "How much fun did I have, and was I kind to myself and others?" It's a beautiful and inspiring perspective to life. She lives this way by nurturing her most cherished relationships, first with herself and then with the ones closest to her.

Let's begin with expectations. As Melissa says, "Expectations ruin relationships." I remember leaning into the microphone after hearing these words, waiting and wanting more because I knew she was right, though I wasn't entirely sure why. I was left wanting to understand Melissa's point better because I had never thought about the expectations I was putting on my relationships. I valued and was grateful for my relationships, but they were on autopilot like most things in life. Some relationships were better than others, and I accepted this, but I never entertained the idea that I could be the one sabotaging these relationships.

Perhaps the relationship I've put the most expectations on and sabotaged the most has been the one I have with myself. As someone who works directly in mental fitness, expecting myself to fix everything shows up in my mental narrative. The expectation that I should have all the mental fitness solutions for myself is something my EVRYMAN men's group (more on this in Dan Doty's profile) often reminds me to release. Sure, I strive to leverage the practices I know work best, but when I release the expectation to have all the answers, a weight lifts off my shoulders, reminding me that I am human just like everyone else.

Take a moment to think of the relationships you cherish most in your life. What expectations are you putting on these relationships? Try this: Write one line per relationship to understand what expectations you have put on the relationship. There is a good chance you have never thought about this, as was the case for me, but taking a few minutes to reflect can change the entire way you show up and experience your relationships from now on. Read the examples below to get started, and do not stop at one expectation. Dive 100% in and list all expectations!

- I expect my *mom and/or dad* to show up this way...
- I expect my *brother and/or sister* to show up this way...
- I expect my *partner* to show up this way...
- I expect my *best friend* to show up this way...
- I expect my *colleagues* to show up this way...
- I expect *myself* to show up this way...

Surprise, surprise! When they don't show up in the way we expect, we are left feeling disappointed, irritated, angry, and frustrated. Melissa is clear and expresses that we need to set and respect our boundaries when going through the exercise. Still, there usually is a lot of room left over to release expectations not serving the relationship.

Going through the exercise first makes us aware of the expectations we are placing on other people, but second, it allows us to release them; all it takes is a conscious decision to let them go. Metaphorically speaking, lift the weight off the relationship to fully enjoy and appreciate the person for who they are. With Melissa's incredible energy, "Show up at every moment. Show up with love. We are here to have a freaking good time in the process!"

What kind of energy am I bringing to my relationships?

Melissa lives life seeking balance, not the work-life balance that has been discussed at length by many, but a balance of masculine and feminine energy. Just as there is no summer without fall, winter, and spring, there are no relationships without masculine and feminine energy, irrespective of your sex.

An important point to note: as you go through the rest of this profile, try not to draw direct correlations between gender and feminine or masculine energies. As a culture, we have messed this one up and still struggle with inequalities. But here, we are talking about consciously identifying and balancing the energy influencing our relationships.

As Melissa says, "Everything is always seeking balance," our masculine and feminine energy being no different. Balancing this energy is a great place to develop, maintain, and propel our relationships forward.

Pause now and think about when you feel your masculine or feminine energy taking over particular situations. What are the scenarios showing up in your life that would benefit from balancing these energies? Doing this reflection in silence, when you're not triggered by a situation requiring an energy change, trains your mind to handle future moments where that shift will be required. The more you consciously train your mind now, the more you will benefit from intuitive energy shifts when you need them most.

Melissa has a simple trigger, or statement, that can help us all be more aware of which energy we are bringing to the conversation: "Speak from your heart, you will reach their heart.

Speak from your head, you will speak to their head." We need both the heart and mind in our relationships. Knowing when and how to balance your energies in all your relationships (romantic, business, and personal) will only bring a more natural flow and pleasant experience.

Am I aware?

Does it not seem like all situations leading to improving ourselves, performing and feeling our best, come right back to heightening our self-awareness? This has to be the case because we can't change, improve, or process if we do not know.

Melissa highlights the importance of "sitting in conversation with yourself," and taking the time to understand the type of energy you are putting into your relationships and knowing when to shift from one energy to another; it can significantly impact our relationships' quality and longevity. These are the micro pauses that many do not take, so you are at an advantage if you are taking them. People will notice. Most importantly, your relationships and how you show up, what you give, and what you can take will be at a new level—the same level where legends and world-class performers operate.

Final Thought

You get what you expect, or don't expect, in your relationships.

What expectations am I holding in my relationships?

What is my inner calling?

Chase Jarvis

World-renowned photographer and entrepreneur

QUICK BIO

- Award-winning artist, entrepreneur, and one of the most influential photographers of the past twenty years
- Shot advertising campaigns for companies like Apple, Nike, and Red Bull
- Contributed to the Pulitzer Prize-winning *New York Times* story *Snowfall* and earned an Emmy nomination for his documentary *Portrait of a City*
- Created Best Camera, the first photo app to share images to social networks
- Founder of CreativeLive, where more than ten million students learn photography, video, design, music, and business from the world's top creators and entrepreneurs
- His book *Creative Calling* debuted as an instant national best seller

---

Behind the Question

The first part of Chase's life was spent, as he would describe it, "doing what I should be doing." Much of this "doing what I should be doing" was traced back to a critically defining moment in Chase's childhood: the day he overheard his second grade teacher tell his mom he was better at sports than art, a short conversation that ended up shaping the first half of his life.

This was the moment Chase dropped arts and went all in with sports. From the outside it probably did not look bad because Chase was on his way to earning a professional career as a soccer player. Right before realizing this accomplishment, though, he dropped soccer to then pursue medical school. These are two paths many would dream of. The issue for Chase, however, was they were not *his* paths, they were the paths that seemed easiest to gain the approval of others. "All my life, I'd sought the approval of others, to achieve at any cost. Becoming a doctor seemed like the obvious choice. The only choice. I truly believed that."

It took the sudden passing of his grandfather to understand the life he was living was not the life he desired. "My grandfather's unexpected death woke me up. Losing him reminded me that I'd only ever have one life. If I didn't pursue my calling on this go-around, I never would."

Chase stepped into his intuition. He followed the signs, and as he would say "whispers in the distance," to do what felt right. He knew he wanted to take photos; everything in his gut was leading him down this path. He put in the work, and years later Chase is a highly awarded and recognized sports and commercial photographer, having worked with organizations like Apple, Starbucks, and Nike. He has won awards like the Prix de la Photographie Paris, the Advertising Photographers of America, and the International Photography Awards, to name a few.

But get this, photography is not even his main focus right

now! The online learning platform CreativeLive that he founded ten years ago is taking up the majority of his time and has now reached millions of people. There is a big difference between now and when he was pursuing a professional soccer career and medical school. Chase is not following what he *should* be doing or what others, like his second grade teacher, thought he should be doing. He has pursued and continues to pursue what lights him up and sparks him out of bed each day.

Where am I playing it safe?

Be honest with yourself and think of the areas in your life where you are playing it safe or following the default path. I understand. I was also on the default path and it actually felt pretty great. It took an enormous life disruption—the unraveling of my journaling app KYO—to fully understand the right path for me.

Society in general also leads us down a preprogrammed path providing what seems like safety and certainty, but in the end if it's not what lights you up, it ends up being a path of frustration and resistance. You may think you are already happy with how your life is unfolding, and that is freaking awesome. I challenge you to sit with that a moment before skipping ahead. Answer the questions for clarity.

A question can serve as the disruptor or wake up moment like Chase had when his grandfather passed. There is also zero downside to spending time reflecting on where you might be playing it safe versus years of your life potentially going by before that moment naturally occurs and a major life pivot is required. Take a few moments for yourself and reflect on the most important areas of your life to understand how you got there and if it's where you want to be.

What is my imagination telling me?

Before jumping into creativity, we first have to reimagine it because we have been given a perception of creativity that is wildly misguided. Does the starving artist, French painter, or photographer living out of his/her van ever come to mind when thinking of a creative career? Yes, I'm also guilty of this, but thankfully Chase can open up a whole new perspective.

> *"Creativity is a critical human function. It imbues every incident we experience in life—every sight, sound, and texture—with profound meaning. Without acknowledging and exercising our creativity in small, consistent ways, we're undermining our natural capacity to imagine, design, execute, and amplify the life we're meant to be living." —Chase Jarvis*

Chase wrote *Creative Calling*, outlining a system centered around imagining, designing, executing, and amplifying your life through creativity. I want to focus on the "imagine" part to help us understand where we might be playing it safe in life. If we can imagine our big dream, then we can understand if our current environment is supporting or holding us back from realizing that dream.

We all know that life can be cut short, so why not work toward our big dream? What do we have to lose? I know what we do have to lose when we are not working toward that dream—time. Time we will wish we had back when we do get to the point of realization. This is the same point Chase came to years after going down the path others programmed for him.

Alright, it's time for a fun journaling exercise, an exercise that has zero limits and is designed to work your creative muscles. Pick up a pen and paper, or take a long walk alone, and imagine a big dream or something you truly want to create and be remembered for. Describe the situation in full detail including how it makes you feel. Reflect on how far or how close you may be to realizing this dream. This is the first step that most of the population never takes while continuing to live a programmed life set out *for* them, not *by* them.

At this point in the profile, clarity should be surfacing for you. Whether you like or do not like what is surfacing, it does not matter; it only matters that something is surfacing. Take a moment to be grateful for these insights and for the work you put in to help them emerge because now you have the opportunity to take action by leveraging this knowledge and moving forward on your own terms.

It's never too late to stop the autopilot. I'm writing this book—loaded full of prompts and profiles of stunning humans—to hopefully help save us all some of that valuable time. As Chase says beautifully, "The end goal isn't the creation of a masterpiece; it's the making of a masterpiece of your life."

Final Thought

Our calling in life can come to us at any point, but tapping into our imagination can save years of discovery.

What is my inner calling?

What do I feel?

Dan Doty

Guides men into deep somatic experiences and emotional maturity

QUICK BIO

- Guides men, leaders, and organizations to feel and express the entirety of their potential
- Creative founder of EVRYMAN with the mission: We can't change what life brings. We can change how we respond
- Dan and EVRYMAN have been featured by *TEDx*, *Inc.*, *Showtime*, *Men's Health*, *The New York Times*, *GQ*, and the *Today Show*
- Former director of hit TV show *MeatEater*, and a longtime wilderness guide
- Has logged 15,000+ hours with men in intense transformation settings
- Three-time guest on *The Joe Rogan Experience*

Behind the Question

It was early morning, still dark outside, and I could hear freezing rain bouncing off the metal roof of the cabin situated in the Berkshires of Massachusetts. I did not know it then, but the man with a podcast mic in front of his face, dimly lit by a small table lamp, had just changed my life. He gave me a gift that years later would pull my life out of a tailspin.

Through support from EVRYMAN, a group of like-minded men come together regularly to share their lives. The gift is being able to truthfully answer the opening prompt and to understand where my feelings are showing up in my body. This group of men does not hold judgement, but holds space for me to get out of my mind and into my body. I meet with my men's group twice a month, but the effects of feeling aware, in control, clear, supported, and loved show up daily.

I'm speaking directly to the men reading this profile because I can relate to you, but for all the women reading this, you will find value in the prompts as well. For the most part, men were raised to not feel, cry, or show emotion, but to be strong no matter what the cost. We have done just that. We are masters at burying our feelings and leveraging our minds to outsmart (at least we think) any situation. After years of putting up protective walls to block any situation from sparking an emotional reaction, we start to go numb. For some men, they stop feeling emotion altogether, good or bad. For others, it's a gradual numbing that can continue for years, decades, or a lifetime.

I attended the EVRYMAN weekend retreat along with fifty other men. It was the first time Dan Doty's father attended an EVRYMAN retreat and the first time Dan could connect with his father's feelings while genuinely getting to know the person he was, inside and out. Dan was thirty-six years old at the time, and he told me, "It was one of the most important events of my entire life." The following scene played out with Dan Doty and his father. While standing one foot apart, eyes locked, Dan's father shared how he felt, where he felt it in his body, and expressed the guilt he held for not sharing those feelings sooner. Dan later mentioned to me that what we all saw was "locked up" his entire life.

I can attest that feelings and emotions were felt because along with Dan and his father, the rest of us were in tears witnessing the two men fully connecting for the first time. Witnessing decades' worth of armor shed in the matter of minutes was one of the most moving experiences I have ever been a part of, reminding me of how powerful one question can be.

I would be remiss to not share the feelings of sadness I later felt in my heart knowing that I could never have that same experience with my father who had recently passed. My dad and I had a great relationship but he no doubt wore protective armor, and I wish I could have experienced what was behind it and connect at another level. If your dad is still around, don't let the opportunity slip by to truly connect. It may look different from the examples shared with Dan and his father; but if something is activated in your body right now and emotions are firing, there is a good chance something has been left unsaid.

Spending time reflecting on how you feel and where you feel it in your body can be used in essentially any situation. This same opening prompt is used every two weeks in my men's group and has allowed me to process the most challenging periods of my life. It's my turn to pass this gift to you. You deserve the opportunity to feel.

Let's get to work. Take a few deep breaths. Inhale for four seconds, hold for four seconds, and exhale for four seconds to calm your mind and relax (a box breathing technique). Write how you are feeling. It is not how you would answer when someone casually asks, "How are you?" Get honest with yourself and write it out. Avoid qualifiers like, "I feel a little bit angry." Fuck that, get to the raw truth: "I feel angry." Own the feeling for what it's worth. All emotions play a role in our lives and can serve as guiding beacons along our journey.

As soon as you feel your mind taking over by intellectualizing your emotions, pause, take a deep breath, close your eyes, and connect with your body. Think about where in your body you feel the emotion. Keep breathing through it and visualize the feelings you want flowing out of your body as you exhale. When you inhale, breathe in how you want to feel. See those emotions coming in through your nose like a wave of energy showering your entire body. Then, open your eyes and finish the practice by listing the awesome things in your life right now.

We spend most of our days up in our heads, but if we can slow down and connect with our body, a new level of awareness and guidance opens up. Dan says it best, "My heart tells me where to go and what to do, my brain is there to figure out how to do it."

What is my heart saying?

Let's tap further into the heart by understanding what's not being said. The theme you are most likely witnessing in all of the profiles revolve around surfacing more data—your internal data. The more we allow time for stillness and reflection, the more data and insights we have to then take action.

Think of the answers you are seeking right now, or a time when you were blocked. Dan's go-to in these situations is the floor. "When I'm stuck on something, I've learned to stop trying so hard and [lie] on the damn floor, and let go for twenty minutes." As you can see, Dan gets quiet, clears out the noise surrounding a situation, and eliminates the unnecessary.

You are probably thinking, "How do I do this?" One answer

is by getting quiet. That's twenty minutes on the floor in silence for Dan, but for you it might be a walk outside with no music, podcasts, or audiobooks—just walk and keep walking until answers start surfacing. When we eliminate complexity and distractions from the equation, clarity surfaces, It becomes easier to hear and trust what your heart is telling you. What feels right for you as a next step? Doty says, "When we trust our experiences and feelings, and we go with it, and we just dive in, the understanding comes."

Where is my safe place?

To go deep, and truly connect with our inner selves, we need a safe place to do this, a place that allows us to be vulnerable and where judgement is not a factor.

Dan's work through EVRYMAN is instantly transformative and, I believe, why men feel compelled to start a local men's group after attending an EVRYMAN retreat, exactly what transpired after my experience in the Berkshires. To create a safe space to connect, there is a set of agreements that each man verbally accepts before any words are ever spoken: agreeing not to judge when another man speaks, listening and empathizing versus trying to fix, and leaving what is shared in the room. When the agreements are set and trust is established, true expression is possible. This can change everything, just as Dan and the rest of us witnessed through his father opening up for the first time in Dan's thirty-six years of being his son.

I want to let you in on a secret and another excellent safe place, a place that can hold tremendous value each day if you apply the same rules and criteria mentioned above. Some people call this place a journal. I call it a place wherever it feels right for you to capture your thoughts. That could be in a notebook, app, audio notes, or something else. I don't care about the tool as long as the reflection is present. We can set those same agreements just mentioned with ourselves as we reflect and unpack our emotions. Even if you have been journaling for years, take the time to list the rules for your reflective space.

Here are mine as an example:
1. I will be kind to myself.
2. I will not hold judgement on my reflections.
3. What is said in my journal stays in my journal unless I decide otherwise.
4. There are no rules (grammar or structure). Just write.

By setting rules and stating your intentions you break down the walls that may have held you back for years. As we continue to create space for ourselves, the best part is that we can then show up for others. As Dan says, "We can only be there for others if we [do] our own deep diving and make room."

Final Thought

Get out of your head and into your body.

Special thanks to my EVRYMAN group: Thank you Nathan and the three Matts (it does get confusing). I appreciate you.

What discomfort am I running from?

Chris Messina

Invented the #hashtag social movement

QUICK NOTES

- Invented the #hashtag which Twitter originally dismissed as being too "nerdy"
- Opened one of the first coworking spaces in the world, kicking off a global shift in how how we work today
- Product designer and speaker for social technology, product design, culture, and mental fitness
- Product therapist helping founders and makers nail their launches on Product Hunt
- Quoted in media outlets such as *The New York Times*, *Businessweek*, *LA Times*, *Washington Post*, and *Wired*
- Appeared in *The Social Dilemma* on Netflix and in books like *No Filter* by Sarah Frier, and *Billion Dollar Loser* by Reeves Wiedeman

---

Behind the Question

The opening prompt was derived from a series of reflective questions Chris left with me during our podcast interview:

- What is this all about?
- What is it all for?
- Why is it so uncomfortable to *not* know?

Chris has been at the forefront of the biggest movements of our time. From inventing the hashtag to being part of creating the first coworking space, he is a well respected and regarded product designer and advisor for social technology. However, he found himself mentally exhausted from asking himself and friends questions in order to avoid the uncomfortable feeling of not knowing. He also found himself stressed by not having all the solutions, data, and/or seeing the next steps. Sound familiar? Yeah, me too. It can be very tiring, or as Chris stated, "I was tight in my mind; it was exhausting." Thankfully, we can leverage great questions to loosen and free up our mental exhaustion.

Take a few minutes to reflect on the discomfort in your life right now. Is the discomfort truly about *this* moment? What factors are contributing to your discomfort? Do not stop there. Keep asking and unpacking what is behind each answer. The goal is to move past the surface and uncover the real source of discomfort. Now for the punchline. Let this all sit in your mind. If the next steps are not clear—do nothing. Yes, you heard me correctly, do nothing.

Chris left excellent insight around the notion of trusting your mind to do the work. He used the example of having "nurtured his soil" and after many successful harvests, the soil is fertile and will produce another crop—when we trust the process. Our mind is full of knowledge and is incredibly powerful.

It can form the connections, insights, and solutions we seek if we give it space to do the work. To use Chris's words, "You are working out a thought splinter." Allow things to come up, and when they do, take action.

How can I access my child-like curiosity?

We are born limitless, free of judgment, and with full curiosity. Just in learning how to walk, we have to experiment, push boundaries, and take risks. As we continue to experience life, restraints and limitations are put onto us. Often, these restraints keep us safe, but over time, they shape our way of living and thinking, a method of thinking that accepts what is in front of us at face value. As a father to a four-year-old boy, I know *nothing* is taken at face value at his age.

Organizations pay consultants hundreds of thousands of dollars to lead teams through exercises of asking "Why?" until true answers surface, but what if we all stepped back into our four-year-old level of curiosity? Or maybe, instead, we bring in a four-year-old to run a strategy session! Many questions would be asked!

Chris decided to leave everything behind in San Francisco to rekindle his childlike curiosity as a digital nomad. Being someone who always worked with technology, relying on data and testing, he wanted to slow down his analytical mind and connect to feeling. It was time to shut off the autopilot and the intensity that came with it: "I was very much 'intensed' out." After making the decision, Chris already felt lighter. However, he was not living a fairy tale and traveling the world without any worry or uncertainty. He felt like he was jumping out of a plane and building the parachute on the way down. He trusted his nourished soil and knew that everything would work out.

He allowed himself to step outside of working *on* social technology and community-driven innovation to *experience* them in the physical world. In 2005, Chris wrote a blog post titled, *The cult of the vagabond hacker*, envisioning a new way of work and life.

> *"I envision cults of travelling hackers, venturing from one city to the next, wardriving and shacking up at homes and offices, seeking caffeine, a decent work environment and space for sleeping bags. Such places need not be permanent destinations, but rather convenient, temporary quarters for such hacking gatherings." —Chris Messina*

Fourteen years later, at a cafe in Lisbon, Portugal, Chris read a direct message from one of his Twitter followers asking if he was sitting at the table across from her. She was a freelance designer that he had previously supported on Product Hunt. She asked him if he wanted to come back to her coworking space. At that moment, without the busyness of his past San Francisco life occupying his mind, he realized he was living *in* the environment he had predicted. The environment that over a decade ago was imagined from his childlike curiosity.

Think about how you can cultivate childlike curiosity in your life. Prioritize the activities and reflective practices in your routine that spark curiosity and thought. Schedule them in your calendar and watch yourself and your ideas multiply.

Where can I let go?

Chris's situation may seem extreme. He packed everything, got rid of his permanent address, and left for unknown locations around the world. By letting go in the physical world, he realized that there was also a mental release taking place. To financially survive while traveling and working around the world, he had to physically let go of things. He realized, though, he had to trust that the memories and thoughts currently fuelling him would come back when he needed them most. Like the physical objects in his life, he let go of the mental narratives to fully lean into this new chapter.

Reflect on the things you are holding onto that no longer serve you. The narratives, relationships, ideas, judgements, and physical things—let them go. Close your eyes and visualize them floating away with only what matters most in your life remaining. We accumulate "a lot of stuff" over the years, physically and mentally. Take inventory of what you have in your life. Understand what is helping you and what might be holding you back. Sometimes refreshing a room in your home can freshen up your mind as well. Take a few minutes to reflect on where you can do a physical or mental "cleanup" to lighten your life.

Final Thought

Your physical and mental worlds are linked; changing one affects the other.

What discomfort am I running from?

How do I protect my soul?

Marcus Aurelius

The Philosopher King

April 26, 121 AD – March 17, 180 AD

QUICK BIO

- Emperor of Rome from 161-180 AD and stoic philosopher
- Widely known for his philosophical teachings preserved in his personal journals titled *Meditations*
- His time as emperor was marked by war and disease with battles over the lands of the East, and the Antonine Plague which devastated the Roman Empire by taking the lives of over five million people
- Known as the last of the Five Good Emperors of the Roman Empire, an age of relative peace and stability

---

Behind the Question

Marcus Aurelius is my spiritual and stoic philosophy guru. It blows my mind to read his reflections from over 2,000 years ago and witness how we are all still in mental combat with the same set of emotions and thoughts. Back in 121 AD they also had to manage fear, loss, anxiety, and they longed for breaks by way of vacations. Marcus Aurelius wrote: "...everything has always been the same and keeps recurring, and it makes no difference whether you see the same things recur in a hundred years or two hundred, or in an infinite period." I believe Marcus Aurelius was able to come to these realizations and many others because of his robust mental fitness regimen (more on this soon).

Let's first set some context because we could easily slip into a school of thought that the world was just different and less complicated 2,000 years ago, that the same stresses of today did not exist back then. True, but not really. Marcus Aurelius lived and ruled as emperor when the Antonine Plague existed, wiping out an estimated five million people. He was away from his family for years on end, fighting in gruesome wars, and having to process the death of eight of his children. As a father, I cannot fathom processing this emotion even once, let alone multiple times. How did he do it? How did he not crumble under the pressures of his time?

He had many practices, but there was one that clearly helped guide Marcus Aurelius through the toughest of times: the belief system fuelling his soul. He had a guiding philosophy helping to maintain perspective, remain calm, and stay connected to a higher meaning and purpose. Marcus Aurelius reflected, "Then what can guide us? Only philosophy." He then went on to describe the significance of philosophy in his life:

"Which means making sure that the power within stays safe and free from assault, superior to pleasure and pain, doing nothing randomly or dishonestly and with imposture, not dependent on anyone else's doing something or not doing it."

Having a belief system to fall back on allows for a momentary pause to think, to shift our perspective from emotionally charged situations to ground us in our belief system and what matters in our lives. I am not saying you should subscribe to stoic philosophy as your guiding belief system, but more so that you *understand* what belief system you are subscribed to and if it works for you. I have four core statements, perspectives, I live by, and they are constantly reinforced by my belief systems:

1. Focus on what I can control (stoic philosophy)
2. Live the present to the max, especially during challenging times (stoic philosophy)
3. My thoughts can shift energy and outcomes in my life (quantum physics)
4. Always be kind (my parents)

We are all born pure with a clean slate, and our belief systems are put upon us as we grow and experience life. Some good, others bad. Regardless, we become our own person, flow through life in various ways, and change from year to year. At some point, we owe it to ourselves to check in with our belief systems. First, understand what they are, and second, to ensure they are still relevant to the person we are or the person we are striving to become.

Try this out: Start with thinking about the belief systems that were imposed upon you while growing up. I am not suggesting these are good or bad; for the most part we had little choice over these belief systems. Reflect on which of those beliefs still hold up and feel right to you today. Now, it's up to us. We have the control and the opportunity to bring in the belief system(s) that will serve us best—throw away any beliefs that no longer apply and list your new ones.

Be patient and kind to yourself because it has taken years to build up your current belief system. Be open, accepting, and willing to experiment and learn about different religions, philosophies, and lenses to view life through. You can turn to the people you admire for inspiration. I was not raised in a household of stoic philosophers. Still, many of the people I admire, such as best-selling authors Tim Ferriss and Ryan Holiday subscribe to stoic philosophy, which inspired me to learn more and now serves me well by training my focus and attention daily on what I can control. Find what works for you and what feels right at this moment in your life. When you find that core belief or operating system, you are gifted with the tools to win in spiritual combat.

What are my spiritual combat practices?

Our belief systems can serve as critical daily reminders and can act as mental fitness on their own. Simply put, we need these daily reminders to protect our minds from the toxicity that unfortunately surrounds us all the time.

I'm an optimist by nature, but I also cannot ignore the facts. We are surrounded by negativity (e.g. the news), and an endless amount of content, deadlines, and work stimulating our minds in unhealthy ways. It's no wonder the majority of the population suffers from chronic stress and disease. Imagine going to the gym to do a high-intensity workout for eight to ten hours straight, five days (sometimes seven days) a week. Does this not sound exhausting and unsustainable? Well, this is precisely the type of workout we put our minds through all week.

The point of my rant is that if left on autopilot we will be steered toward unhealthy places. This shows up in many ways such as insomnia, fatigue, substance misuse, chronic disease, and the list goes on. Thankfully, we have access to preventative training, Marcus Aurelius's most prized practice, and what Ryan Holiday and other scholars have called "spiritual combat." This is the very thing we are doing together throughout *Personal Socrates*—journaling, or intentional reflection.

The practice keeps us in check and present with our belief systems to navigate and process the daily stresses. Without this reflection, the eight-hour high-intensity workout can go unnoticed until it's too late and physical symptoms of the problem stop us in our tracks. With our belief systems identified and guiding us, it's now all about staying present with those systems. Implement reminders and practices like journaling, meditation, visualization, and reading to remind us that we have everything required to process any and all situations.

The small daily practices make all the difference. For example, I was working one-on-one with a high-performing entrepreneur, and it was not until she created space for micro reflections throughout the day that she then realized, "I am tense the majority of the day." With the tension identified, we can work on releasing it and deploy practices to minimize future tension. This is the power of journaling and intentional reflection.

My morning coffee ritual, which includes one reading from *The Daily Stoic* by Ryan Holiday, always primes my mind with a refreshed perspective to the narrative running through my head at the time. Without that reminder, which triggers my belief system, I run the risk of starting the day with a destructive looping narrative. Instead, I can release the story and start the day on my terms.

Perhaps the most powerful tool I have ever come across, and the very practice that guides me through my most challenging times, is entirely dropping into the present moment. When I think of spiritual combat, this is *the* tool and method that can diffuse anything. And, I am constantly reminded of this through Marcus Aurelius's teachings:

> *"Forget everything else. Keep hold of this alone and remember it: Each of us lives only now, this brief instant. The rest has been lived already, or is impossible to see. ...if you can embrace this without fear or expectation—can find fulfillment in what you're doing now, as Nature intended, and in superhuman truthfulness (every word, every utterance)— then your life will be happy. No one can prevent that."*

We all have equal access to this superpower. All it takes is focus on the now and a place where you can breathe through tension, be grateful for the moment in front of you, and be reminded of what guides you.

Final Thought

When we train and strengthen our minds, we protect our souls by default.

PART TWO

Live Intentionally

As we get clearer, we notice our reactions and how our thoughts, emotions, and relationships predict our results. We see how these elements affect our mood, mindset, and behavior. We come to the realization that we have a choice: intentionally design our life or allow others to design it for us. The choice is ours, and it starts with the questions we ask to design the life we want to live.

The profiles and prompts in part two will stimulate reflection to live and act with intention leading us to realize our greatest desires, passions, and dreams.

How do I get to the rim?

Kobe Bryant

One of the greatest NBA players of all time

August 23, 1978 – January 26, 2020

QUICK BIO

- Retired from the NBA in 2016 having played twenty seasons with the Los Angeles Lakers
- Won five NBA titles, scored the most points in one game (60) by any player in the 2015 - 2016 season
- Left the game with 33,643 regular season points—third most all-time behind Kareem Abdul-Jabbar and Karl Malone
- Focused on giving back, teaching the game, and bringing the lessons of basketball to the masses through storytelling during his retirement
- Won an Academy Award (2018) for Best Animated Short Film for *Dear Basketball*
- His life, along with his thirteen-year-old daughter and seven others, was cut short in a tragic helicopter crash on January 26, 2020

*"Without hoops, I would not understand
how to create or write, I would not understand human
nature, nor would I know how to lead. The game, in essence,
taught me the art of storytelling. Without it, I would not
have an Emmy, I would not have an Oscar." —Kobe Bryant*

Behind the Question

We are all expert internal negotiators. We can justify a million different ways to get ourselves out of an early morning workout. It's raining outside, so I'll wait until the weather clears up for my run. I'll eat healthy all day and get my workout in first thing tomorrow instead. I pushed it too hard yesterday, so today I need to rest. Insert whatever internal narrative(s) you tell yourself to negotiate out of the things that are hard to show up for consistently. Be honest with yourself—what do you talk yourself out of?

Kobe realized early on that the most important conversations he could have would be with himself. He set his alarm to wake up at four o'clock each morning allowing for an additional training session from his peers. It was not easy. Kobe had that same "little voice" trying to talk himself out of it each day. The difference with Kobe from many, he paused the internal narrative and got up. Kobe lived by the "mamba mentality," a term he made up and defined as, "a constant quest to be better today than you were yesterday." We will come back to the mamba mentality soon, but first let's talk about motivators.

He had a clear motivator driving him daily to get out of bed: winning the NBA Championship. What is your motivator? Write it down and see and feel yourself accomplishing that goal. Making it real in your head first will help shut down the internal negotiations that may hold you back from crossing the finishing line.

As I write these words, the sense of accomplishment of publishing and holding my first book in my hands is my motivator. Each morning I write. Some mornings I feel like writing, others I don't, but I still write each morning. I am human and also a master internal negotiator. I can easily talk myself out of writing in the morning. "I'm not feeling creative this morning, so I'll write in the afternoon to produce a better result." The afternoon shows up, and guess what? I don't write because life happens, things come up, and I run out of time.

Winning the NBA Championship likely is not your motivator (if it is, hell yeah!), but we all have our own motivators. Find what will drive you and use it to stop the internal negotiation before it goes too far because you know that little voice will prevail if it's given enough time to do so.

Television host, motivational speaker, and author Mel Robbins has an incredible tool to cut the negotiation in its tracks— the 5,4,3,2,1 countdown. As soon as your internal negotiation starts, countdown from five then get out of bed, or turn the water to cold in the shower, and take the action you were trying to negotiate yourself out of taking. We should never underestimate the power of our minds. When we decide to do something, we can defy a multitude of limiting beliefs. As illustrated in Kobe's words:

"You pull your hamstring and can barely walk.
Your only option is to rest and heal. But as you sit in your
house, with your spouse and kids, a fire erupts. I guarantee
you will sprint up the stairs, grab your kids, and run out of
the house without thinking about your pulled hamstring."

What does my self-talk sound like?

It was 2008—Kobe and the Los Angeles Lakers had just lost in the NBA finals to the Boston Celtics. That evening, in his hotel room, Kobe was furious and questioned everything. He thought to himself, "I may never win another championship, maybe it's not in the cards to win again." Not the self-talk you would expect from one of the greatest basketball players of all time. But, like us, Kobe was human.

The next morning, however, was a very different internal narrative. The story shifted from anger and hopefulness to a set of questions:

- Where did we go wrong?
- Why did we lose?
- How am I going to lead this team differently?

The following year the Lakers won the NBA Championship against the Orlando Magic, and in 2010, won against the Boston Celtics. It's not about repressing thoughts and emotions, it's about feeling them and then moving on from a negative narrative. For Kobe that morning, it was changing the set of questions that made all the difference.

Whom do I need to study?

While most people admired Michael Jordan for his high scoring and fancy dunks, Kobe Bryant was asking one question: How is he getting to the rim? Kobe studied Jordan's footwork, pacing, and the fundamentals that made him who he was. Often we only see or celebrate the outcomes of the work, championships, IPOs, or rewards. The magic, though, lives in the prompts beginning with how and what. These questions unlock the mysteries that most are unwilling to solve—how and what was required to get to the final outcome.

Take a few minutes to list the people who inspire you, and start asking questions. What have they done that inspires you? What did they do to get to that level? When taking the time to reflect and dissect your heroes, you'll save hours, days, and potentially years of searching how to be world class. There are many books and podcasts on the subjects, but the answers lay right in front of us, through the people we respect.

How can I outwork myself?

On January 26, 2020, we lost Kobe Bryant in a tragic helicopter crash. He gave his heart and soul to basketball, and many will continue to benefit from his contributions to the sport well past the forty-two years he spent with us. But, he also leaves us with a specific mindset and way of life—mamba mentality, striving to make each day better than the last.

In retrospect, after reviewing past interviews and studying the questions he asked himself and others, the mamba mentality is quite apparent in everything Kobe did. He was known for outworking his competitors, but he also applied this same mentality to himself: "You always want to outwork your potential." His biggest competitor was himself, and he deployed the mamba mentality to grow each day. Reflective questions were at the core of Kobe genuinely living this way of life. His goals and the vision he had for himself were crystal clear:

- What do I enjoy doing?
- If I could work hard every single day, what would my career look like?
- What can I control?
- What do I want to work on first?

- Is this the best I can do?

What I like about the mamba mentality is its universal application. It's not a basketball mentality, it's a life mentality that we can all leverage no matter what we are pursuing. Take the time to be clear in what you want for yourself, study those who are the best, and outwork your potential to grow each day.

Final Thought

What legends have achieved is far less important than *how* they have achieved it.

Who am I optimizing to become?

James Clear
Habits and systems expert

QUICK BIO

- Author of the *New York Times* best-selling, *Atomic Habits*, which has sold well over four million copies worldwide
- Work revolves around five main topics:
  - How to start (and stick to) good habits
  - How to make good choices and avoid bad ones
  - How to accomplish more in less time
  - How to create better systems and processes
  - How to achieve meaningful results without overwhelming yourself
- Has one of the most thought-provoking email newsletters I have ever received
  (one million plus subscribers)
- Weightlifter with a 501-pound deadlift
- Was an ESPN Academic All-American baseball pitcher in college
- Donates 5 percent of his profits to the Against Malaria Foundation each year

---

Behind the Question

Often we optimize our days, schedules, and time to be the most productive as humanly possible, but is this optimization focused in the right areas? Are we dedicating our time to activities leading to the person we want to become or leading us entirely in the other direction? As James would ask, "Am I climbing the right mountain?" It's easy to climb, to push forward, and to trick ourselves into feeling accomplished. It's harder to pause and truly reflect on whether that mountain, the promotion, or the new city is the right move for us. These types of questions are challenging because they are hard to answer, or I should say, the answers are hard to accept.

The faster we can be honest with ourselves by asking tough questions, the sooner we will be pointed in the direction of our desired outcomes. You might be thinking, "I am on the right path," which may be accurate; but there is a chance you *think* you are on the right path, but spending time with great questions may reveal you are not. This is completely okay. Life is an adventure with many stages; we can enjoy them all.

> *"You're not going to get your identity nailed in one go."*
> —James Clear

Thinking of your identity or whom you want to become might feel overwhelming and grandiose, but it's manageable if you break it down into smaller steps. Start with reflecting on what makes you feel happy, alive, and gives you meaning in your life. Then, fall into James's world of forming habits and systems that fuel the person you want to become.

If you want to write a book but are not in the habit of writing each day, then there is a disconnect. If you want to look and feel healthier, but are in the habit of starting each day with unhealthy choices, then there is a disconnect. Your habits are either supporting the person you want to become or they are not. As our lives continually evolve we also need to ensure our habits evolve at the same rate. As prompted by James, "Can my current habits carry me to my desired future?"

A byproduct of being consciously aware of what you are optimizing for is the ability to prioritize focus. When you know where to focus, you also know where *not* to focus. You know which meetings to take or which opportunities are the right opportunities.

When James's book *Atomic Habits* started taking off, he was inundated with opportunities, which sounds like a perfect situation. He put in years' worth of work and was now reaping the rewards. But there were problems in this situation—physically and mentally. Like us, James only has twenty-four hours in a day and could not physically be in all of the locations presenting opportunities. The situation presented a mental hurdle for him because not too long ago just one of those opportunities would have been the most significant thing to happen to him, and now they were showing up in multitudes.

How did James say no to opportunities that a month before would have been game-changing for his life? He followed the advice in his own book and paused to reflect on the person he was trying to optimize for. He then assessed the opportunities that would best support that person. James's example might not be the norm, but remember he too was on the other side of the words not long ago, learning just as you are right now. With that being said, his principles can be widely applied to various situations.

How often have you been faced with opportunities that seemed fantastic and you knew you were already stretched thin, yet you still pushed forward? We all know what comes next—overwhelm. And when we are operating in a state of overwhelm, we are not performing at our best. Our minds are cluttered, and we can't see the signs in front of us. Also, we generally don't feel great along the way. One simple pause ensuring the opportunity in front of you optimizes and supports the person you want to become can make all the difference.

How do I balance consumption versus creation?

As my conversation continued with James, I absolutely needed to understand one thing. I wanted to know what habits and systems supported his ability to surface world-class thoughts and content. His weekly newsletter (3-2-1) is something I read, then mark as unread, to incorporate into my next morning's journaling and mental fitness. It's that damn good.

I followed my curiosity and was met with James's 80/20 rule for creation: 20 percent consumption and 80 percent creation. You can't create without consumption or inspiration, but too much consumption will get you nowhere. The rule is simple and makes perfect sense, but then why is it so easy to overconsume? Because it's easier to consume than to create. Creating, or doing the work, is hard. It takes effort, challenges us, and can be uncomfortable.

When I decided to snowboard for the first time, I immediately went to YouTube for help. I did not want to be that guy who stops the lift for everyone else because I fell down trying to get off the chair, or the guy flailing around the whole way down the hill. After hours of how-to videos, I thought of James and was reminded that I was overconsuming and needed to drop my fear of being judged and get on the hill to practice. As covered in Kobe Bryant's profile, we can negotiate ourselves out of anything. I just needed one more video on how to carve on my snowboard, one more video on...and then I would feel ready. No—what I needed was to get on the hill to practice and create experiences that I could then learn from.

Creating content, brand strategies, and *name your example* are no different. Take 20 percent of your time to consume and learn, but then put yourself out there and create. During the 20 percent consumption period, make sure you are consuming quality content. Otherwise garbage in, garbage out. What you consume dictates what you will produce. Trust your mind to make the connections and surface only the best insights. As James noted, "Let the very best ideas funnel through." This is exactly what I am doing with these profiles—funnelling through the best prompts, practices, and ideas for all of us to incorporate into our lives.

Ask yourself: How often am I consuming versus creating, and is what I am consuming of the highest quality? Now take a pause from consuming this profile and go create!

Is there a better way to do this?

The theme of curiosity and example of "poking at the sides of the box" continually surfaced during my interview with James. There is an underlying notion that he does not accept the default. As he continued the process of writing his first book, he was consistently asking his publishing team: "Is there a better way to do this?" With the response often being, "No one has ever asked that question before."

By default, if you're asking good questions and pushing the status quo, you are in the top percentage of thinkers; most are not motivated to jump off the easy path. Not accepting the default and having the self-awareness to pause and ask a question may seem overly simplistic, but it's not. Most people are driven to be productive in our hyper productivity-oriented society which often shows up as the illusion of efficiency and completing as many tasks as possible throughout the day. That system does not allow for the pause to question because questioning slows down the process and volume output. See Chip Conley's profile for more on this topic.

If you can leverage the practices and prompts in this book to slow down and train your mind to think and be curious, the quality of your output will increase substantially. It is no accident that James is a *New York Times* best-selling author having sold millions of books. James seeks to understand and strives to improve what is in front of him. It's a formula that will always lead to opportunity, but not just any opportunity—the right opportunity. He understands where to ask better questions and where to direct his energy to support the person he is optimizing to become, a formula that we all have access to. Think about where you are choosing the easy path and where you can "poke the box" with intentional curiosity.

Final Thought

Filter projects, relationships, and opportunities based on whom you are striving to become.

Am I standing up or sitting down?

Rosa Parks

Mother of the freedom movement

February 4, 1913 – October 24, 2005

QUICK BIO

- Civil rights activist who shaped history by refusing to give up her seat to a white passenger on a segregated bus in Montgomery, Alabama, leading to her arrest
- The Montgomery African American community boycotted public transportation for 381 days sparked by Rosa's arrest
- Segregation on public transit was ruled unconstitutional by the Supreme Court following the Montgomery bus boycott
- Awarded the Martin Luther King Jr. Award by the National Association for the Advancement of Colored People, the Presidential Medal of Freedom, and the Congressional Gold Medal
- Worked as a seamstress in a Montgomery department store until losing her job following her arrest
- Created a new life in Detroit, Michigan, working as a receptionist and continued her civil rights pursuits
- In 1999 she was among *TIME* magazine's list of "The 20 Most Influential People of the 20th Century"

Behind the Question

Rosa Parks lived in a world that forced African Americans to get on a bus at the front, pay their fare, walk off the bus, and re-board from the back. It's shocking to think human beings were treated in this way. I realize there are many worse examples that could be shared, and that we still have a long way to go, but Rosa Parks's message gives me hope.

"It's far from perfect, and it may never be, but as long as we do the best we can to improve conditions, then more people will be benefited." —Rosa Parks

It starts with us, a decision to pause and reflect on the actions we take each day, just as Rosa Parks did on December 1, 1955. Rosa's decision: "I got on first and paid the same fare, and I didn't think it was right for me to have to stand so someone else who got on later could sit down." Following a 381-day Montgomery Bus Boycott, a ruling declared segregation on public transport unconstitutional.

There is so much we can learn from Rosa Parks; but what struck me was the idea of a system that enforced division, hierarchy, and bias, something that still happens daily in many scenarios.

Are you passing judgement on other people or races? Are you being dismissive with your colleagues or leaving people feeling inferior based on your words and actions? If so, why? There is something behind it. Take time to unpack these motivators. Don't hold back. Release yourself of any judgement. You're here now taking steps to grow and evolve. This is not easy. I'm sending you virtual high fives because if we can do it, we can be a part of the change versus being part of the problem.

In my past life/work, I remember when I spent the majority of my day having conversations with physicians and often feeling like I was the inferior human. I appreciated their specialized knowledge, but often did not feel the same appreciation in return. It was a shitty feeling, and I obviously didn't stick around in that particular line of work.

I'm also guilty of making others feel inferior. Many years ago, the entry of my morning journaling session ended with, "Who the hell do you think you are?" It was eye-opening for me. In my corporate years, I used to work with many suppliers and agencies on a variety of projects. On a few of these projects, I would go in thinking, "I'm the client. I'm paying you. You have to deliver for me." I never said those words aloud, but I might as well have given the way I was acting. I'm ashamed to even share this with you. My journaling revealed I was in over my head in work and deliverables causing quick and emotion-driven reactions. No one ever said anything to me, but I knew, and I never wanted my actions to make someone else feel inferior again.

Imagine your son, daughter, or someone who deeply respects you is standing by your side, observing your every move. Would they be proud of your actions? We can learn from Rosa Parks and apply the same thinking across various situations and topics, including racial and social injustices which unfortunately still exist. If we can reflect on where we can improve, and focus on ensuring the people around us feel equal in all situations, then we can set a new example and have a chance at making real change, just as Rosa Parks did when she decided to remain seated.

What action can I take?

There is a beautiful line from Rosa Parks to remind us how important it is to stand for what we believe in: "Stand for something, or you will fall for anything. Today's mighty oak is yesterday's nut that held its ground." Such a powerful perspective. Everything we see and experience today was once just an idea, thought, or decision that grew into something through action.

Years of dedication from Rosa Parks and her supporters have led to global change. That change continues to grow new oak trees through the Rosa and Raymond Parks Institute for Self Development, making it a priority to inspire and educate our youth so they can make a difference, too. This institute focuses on the youth's self-development by first getting rid of prejudice and ill-will towards other people, then motivating them to reach their highest potential. When we truly believe in something, people take notice, and sometimes all it takes is one push forward, one person to make a decision, that then mobilizes many to join the cause.

It's no different for us. As Jerry Colonna (his profile is coming up) would suggest, we should be reviewing the belief systems we were raised with to understand the flaws and make the changes in support of the person we want to be. When we move toward whom we want to be, while standing up for what we believe in, others will notice and be there in support.

Much has been achieved since Rosa Parks's decision to stay seated on a bus in 1955, but there is still more work to be done. Let's all allow her plight to serve as a reminder of what is possible and to inspire us all to be the best version of ourselves.

> *"Each person must live their life as a model for others."*
> —*Rosa Parks*

Think about what matters to you, but also what matters to others.

Final Thought

Sometimes staying seated is actually taking a stand.

Am I standing up or sitting down?

What is within my control?

Ryan Holiday
Modern day Stoic philosophy expert

QUICK BIO

- Writer, media strategist, and stoic philosophy expert
- Author of multiple best-selling books such as *The Obstacle Is the Way*, *Ego Is the Enemy*, *The Daily Stoic*, *Conspiracy and Stillness is the Key* which have all sold more than two million copies in thirty languages
- Apprentice under globally-renowned author Robert Greene (author of *The 48 Laws of Power*)
- Founder of Brass Check, a creative agency which has advised clients like Google, TASER, and Complex, as well as many prominent best-selling authors, including Neil Strauss, Tony Robbins, Tim Ferriss and *me* for this book (Thanks, Ryan!)
- Lives on a ranch outside Austin, Texas, where he writes between raising cattle, donkeys, and goats

---

The Backstory
I need to give more context to this profile as Ryan has had an

enormous impact on the book you hold in your hands. Who is Ryan Holiday to me? Ryan is a modern-day Stoic. He has served as a mentor for me from afar through his books and teachings and has infiltrated my life (in a good way) with his work. Every morning starts with one passage from Ryan's book *The Daily Stoic*, with the pages yellowing after years of leaning up against my coffee machine in the morning sun. Then there is *Stillness Is The Key*, prominently displayed on my desk, reminding me to slow down and to find the quiet throughout the day.

Perhaps the most significant impact Ryan has had on me comes through the pages you are reading. The way this book is organized and presented to you is a direct result of Ryan Holiday. The first version of the book was structured very differently until Ryan and his partner from Brass Check challenged the 25,000 words I had already written. I started over with a fresh perspective and guidance from people I respect. Ryan continues to fuel and guide my days with perspective and intention through his books, and I am beyond excited to share some of that wisdom with you through the lens of *Personal Socrates*.

Behind the Question

Ryan has written on many topics, but the concept of focusing on what we can control is something he and the stoics before him consistently return to. Learning about Stoicism through Ryan's wealth of knowledge has vastly changed how I live and the lens through which I view life. This lens continues to give me perspective, bulletproofs my mental health, and allows me to be the best person I can be. When I have a question about Stoicism, I skip the Google search and go straight to the expert—Ryan Holiday.

From Ryan's perspective, "Stoicism is a tool in the pursuit of self-mastery, perseverance, and wisdom: something one uses to live a great life, rather than some esoteric field of academic inquiry." It is nearly impossible to operate at our best or pursue "self-mastery" if we are on a rollercoaster of emotions focusing on the things in life that are out of our control. It's challenging and not always intuitive (but it can be through mental training) to dismiss thoughts that drag us into a destructive looping narrative. This thinking leads to forecasting every possible negative outcome to a situation, leaving us feeling fearful, anxious, and far from clear decisions. We are all *New York Times* best-selling authors with the internal stories we create in our minds.

There is an alternative perspective available to us all, one inspired by the stoics and how Ryan lives his life:

> *"That space between your ears—that's yours. You don't just have to control what gets in, you also have to control what goes on in there. You have to protect it from yourself, from your own thoughts. Not with sheer force, but rather with a kind of gentle, persistent sweeping. Be the librarian who says "Shhh!" to the rowdy kids, or tells the jerk on his phone to please take it outside. Because the mind is an important and sacred place. Keep it clean and clear."*

Ryan's words "gentle" and "persistent" are important grounding characteristics that help focus our mind on what we can control. We want to avoid thrashing around aggressively in a state of panic when faced with challenging situations. This survival-centric state of mind is outdated for the times we live in today. I'll take the fight-or-flight program of thinking when my life is literally at risk of ending, but for all other circumstances, I am doing everything possible to keep my mind "clean and clear."

Try this the next time you feel your chest tightening, anger rising, or a whirlwind of thoughts forming. First, take a deep breath. As Ryan says, remember the "librarian who says 'Shhh!' to the rowdy kids…" or in other words, tell your thoughts to keep it down. Then list what is within your control of the situation you are stewing in. Start with how you are deciding to react to the situation at that very moment. Choose to consciously process the situation versus simply responding in the moment with emotion is already a win.

With what you can control identified and emotions calmed, you can now craft a logical plan and take the appropriate actions forward. Processing big decisions or emotionally charged situations using stoic principles can be a huge asset. Living life in its totality through this lens will enrich your daily experiences beyond imagination.

I first started de-escalating thoughts and emotions using this technique in a professional setting, but quickly noticed the spillover into my personal life. Trivial things like being stuck in traffic and watching the estimated arrival time in Google Maps increase by the minute would normally set off anger and anxiety as a person who prides themselves on always being punctual. Through stoic principles and Ryan's teachings, I have been able to calm those situations by accepting what I can control— in this case, my reaction while in the car. Instead of focusing on the traffic (that I can't control), I redirect my attention by checking in to see how my parents are doing, finishing a podcast, or observing the details around me. Taking this approach allows for much more pleasant experiences, not to mention I am not arriving at events with stress and frantic energy.

Here's the kicker! When looking back on the handful of situations when I have been late, I am typically only five or ten minutes late. Had I let my *New York Times* best-selling author's internal narrative be written, the stress, panic, and anxiety associated with that story would have resembled what you would expect—someone showing up hours late or missing the event completely. You can plan all you want, give yourself a comfortable buffer, but oftentimes things are outside your control. Ask yourself, "Is this reaction worth the energy I'm giving it?"

When all else fails, there is one perspective hack we can borrow from Ryan to immediately shift how we react in any situation: our mortality. Ryan carries around a Memento Mori medallion in his pocket, reminding him that he could leave life at any moment. This was a method used by one of Rome's most renowned emperors, Marcus Aurelius, to shift his perspective and avoid reacting emotionally in situations.

Stressing about being five or ten minutes late now seems pretty silly if these could be my last minutes on earth. I know it's extreme, but the perspective shift works. Try it out, and keep your perspective in check.

> *"Our actions, our thoughts, our feelings,*
> *these are up to us. Other people, the weather,*
> *external events, these are not."* — *Ryan Holiday*

How do I nourish my mind?

Many know Ryan Holiday as being a ferocious reader. No exaggeration, he reads hundreds of books per year. When I first realized how much Ryan was reading, I was surprised to learn that he is not some speed-reading anomaly. In fact, he reads quite slowly, given the detailed notes (more on this soon) he takes on each book. Ryan goes straight to the point, "If you want to read more, there's no real secret. It's about adjusting your priorities and your perception so that reading becomes an extension of who you are and what you do."

It's that simple. Prioritize time to read, learn, think, and fuel your mind with the highest quality mental nutrition. Think about what you are consuming daily. We can spend an evening watching endless Netflix dramas or being taught by some of the most significant figures of our world (like many of the legends profiled in this book). It's our decision.

Here's what can happen when filling up our minds with top quality information and wisdom: insights and ideas spark, powerful questions surface, and transparent decisions present themselves. As Ryan says, "The right question at the right time can change the course of a life, can still a turbulent mind, or heal an angry heart." We find those questions, or those questions find us, when we actively seek wisdom and feed our mind with quality mental nutrition.

What is my knowledge system?

Incorporating knowledge and wisdom into action and practical use in daily life is where Ryan truly shines. He has a system initially acquired from his mentor and best-selling author Robert Greene which creates a knowledge database goldmine. You do not have to be a writer to use the system. Anyone can reap the benefits. Here's Ryan's system:

> *"Even though I read hundreds of books every single year,
> I actually read quite slow. In fact, I read deliberate-
> ly slow, so that I can take notes (and then whenever I
> finish a book, I go back through and transcribe these
> notes for my version of a commonplace book...)"*

Ryan's "commonplace book" consists of boxes of 4x6-inch index cards categorically organized to review and use the information when needed. He includes the theme/category on the top right corner to keep the cards organized but also so he can shuffle them around.

He prepares for specific projects or his next book using this method, precisely what he did when writing the bestseller *The Obstacle is The Way*. "I filled out thousands of these cards for ideas and concepts that I wanted included in the book." Some of Ryan's categories include stoicism, life, strategy, and writing. Make sure to use categories that make sense and will be useful for you. The key to the system is that you use it, and you'll use it if it's valuable and practical for your life.

I recently started using this system to capture, retain, and apply the knowledge from what I'm reading because of the research for this profile. I wish I started this sooner! In the short time since implementing it, I've journaled on quotes and captured great thoughts for my next book! The categories I'm using right now include reflective practices, flowing through life, Socratic method, internal narrative, stillness, and focus.

I do have a similar system for collecting powerful reflective questions from everyone I have ever interviewed. I have hundreds of these prompts that I return to for guidance when journaling through big life decisions, processing emotions, or looking for a fresh perspective. Regardless of the system, it's useless if you do not use it. It's no different than an unopened book sitting on your shelf. Try Ryan's analog system or another setup that works with your routine to set yourself up for success.

Where is my stillness?

Get ready to combine two superpowers that will change your world: knowledge and stillness. When I think of someone mastering this combination, I think of Ryan, and based on his books' success, it seems like I'm not the only one.

"If we want to think better, we need to seize these moments of quiet. If we want more revelations—more insights or breakthroughs or new, big ideas—we have to create more room for them. We have to step away from the comfort of noisy distractions and simulations. We have to start listening." — Ryan Holiday

I believe the clarity we seek is born when knowledge meets stillness. This is also the reason I'm encouraging you to take your time reading this book. Stop, journal, and reflect on the prompts and ideas from the profiles as they resonate with your life today. It's amazing what happens when we slow down, take a walk in silence, write in our journal, or just stare out a window. The dust settles, and the path presents itself.

Ryan says it best, "The world is like muddy water. To see through it, we have to let things settle. We can't be disturbed by initial appearances, and if we are patient and still, the truth will be revealed to us." Think of the places and practices that bring you the most stillness. Build them into your weekly routine and allow your mind to spark and connect the dots from all the wisdom and knowledge sitting in your incredible mind.

Final Thought

Life lightens when we focus on what we can control.

Why do I think I know better?

Stephen Hawking

Scientist whose revolutionary discovery enabled the study of black holes

January 8, 1942 – March 14, 2018

QUICK BIO

- Challenged Einstein's theory that nothing could escape a black hole, a theory or controversy known as Hawking radiation
- Director of research at the Centre for Theoretical Cosmology at the University of Cambridge
- Wrote *A Brief History of Time* to open up the quest for a theory of the universe accessible to anyone, which ended up selling over ten million copies
- Diagnosed with amyotrophic lateral sclerosis (ALS) early in life, but never let the disease stop his work or zest for life
- Offered a free flight to space by Sir Richard Branson, which he trained for, but died before it was possible

---

Behind the Question

Questions injected life into Stephen Hawking's mind, body, and spirit for seventy-six years despite being diagnosed with amyotrophic lateral sclerosis (ALS) at the young age of twenty-one. He quickly lost the physical ability to function on his own, being confined to a wheelchair and requiring a computer to communicate. However, the constant search for answers and pushing the boundaries in our understanding of the universe gave him life where many would have given up.

After researching Hawking's life for what seemed like ten minutes but turned out to be several hours, I was left wondering how he was able to accomplish so much while living with one of the most debilitating diseases. I had to understand how someone who was losing control of the muscles required to speak, eat, move, and breathe could continue to be such a prominent figure and contributor to physics and cosmology. The answer then appeared from Stephen himself, "Although my body is very limited, my mind is free to explore the universe."

When I read his words I feel inspired and motivated, and I am reminded that everything starts and stops with our minds. How we decide to react in any situation greatly affects the outcome. We have the wonderful advancement in science, physics, and cosmology because Stephen did not give into ALS and the belief that his life would soon be over after receiving an incurable diagnosis. He did not lose hope, and he kept his mind stimulated and curious.

It shouldn't come as a shock that the Socratic method shows up again. We can see the line of questioning within the opening of his book *A Brief History of Time*:

> *"What do we know about the universe,*
> *and how do we know it? Where did the universe come*

from, and where is it going? Did the universe have a beginning, and if so, what happened before then? What is the nature of time? Will it ever come to an end? Can we go back in time?"

We can all agree these are colossal questions, but what I learned from Stephen is that none of them matter without the opening prompt to this profile. A question like "Why do we *think* we know better?" is the trigger to opening our minds to possibility. Even when what appears in front of us may seem to be true, there can be other explanations leading to new discoveries. Easier said than done because often our ego wants to be right.

Think about a time when you had a disagreement with another person and emotions were flying high. Typically, during the conversation, and even more so post conversation, within our internal narrative we are looking for all the arguments supporting our position to be *right*. What if we let go of being right? We could then approach life and situations, like Stephen, with an open and curious mind and to know that anything is truly possible—just look up into the sky.

Am I looking down at my feet or up at the stars?

Do you remember laying down as a kid and staring up at the stars in complete wonder? There was nothing to worry about, or rush off and do—just you and your wonder for the magical night sky. I remember the peacefulness, the stillness, and the feeling that there is something much bigger than me up there.

Stephen Hawking held onto that same feeling throughout his life. The wonder and curiosity fuelled him, and I personally believe it kept him alive another fifty-five years after being diagnosed with ALS (when the average life expectancy is only three to five years). We greatly underestimate the power of our mind. I remember interviewing a physician around the topic of longevity, and he stated that the most effective treatment when receiving a cancer diagnosis was a positive mindset.

> *"Remember to look up at the stars and not down at your feet. Try to make sense of what you see and wonder about what makes the universe exist. Be curious. And however difficult life may seem, there is always something you can do and succeed at. It matters that you don't just give up." —Stephen Hawking*

These few sentences sum up how Stephen viewed and lived his life. His mind was always pointing up and in wonder even when physically he could not. He once said, "I have been very lucky my disability has not been a serious handicap, indeed, it has probably given me more time than most people to pursue the quest for knowledge." Lucky! I was taken aback when I first heard these words come out of his computer-assisted voice system. To have the mental capacity to view ALS *not* as a massive disability is truly inspiring.

We can all apply this mentality and perspective to our own lives. Take any circumstance or challenge in front of you and think about how you can reframe the situation with your head up and driven to succeed. We spend much of our day naturally looking down because of our electronic devices, so we need to consciously focus on bringing our head up and moving forward in confidence. There is great science backing the relationship of good posture and our mood, but think of it from a practical standpoint. When someone is sad or has low-self esteem, what do you picture in your mind? They are typically hunched over with their face pointing down versus someone who is curious (looking up while thinking), motivated, and excitedly walking around with their chest out, head high, and a smile on their face.

I find it fascinating that someone like Stephen Hawking, who near the end of his life could only twitch his cheek muscle to communicate, is the person inspiring me to write about being conscious of our physical posture. It's a sign of a true legend. Although he was physically limited, his mind stood straight up— curious, confident, and motivated.

Try this: Select a time each day over the next week to look up in wonder. No agenda, objective, or goal—just stop, take a breath, and look up at the sky for five minutes. Thoughts and questions will naturally surface. Let them flow and take note of your thoughts so you can journal on your reflections. You will be surprised at what surfaces when you give your mind time, even for just a few minutes, to wonder. I have found this practice grounding, and I do my best to incorporate a few deep breaths while looking up at the sky in wonder each morning. I always leave this practice feeling refreshed with perspective and reminded that possibility and opportunity is infinite. Let's all remember Stephen Hawking the next time we catch ourselves looking down when we could be looking up.

Final Thought

Questioning the truth reveals that there is always more to discover.

Why do I think I know better?

How will I use my next footstep?

Samantha Gash
Ultra-endurance athlete

QUICK BIO

- Endurance athlete, inspirational speaker, author, social impact entrepreneur, World Vision & Royal Flying Doctor Service Ambassador, and mother
- Raised approximately $1.3 million for charity while advocating for women's empowerment, social change, and access to education
- First female and youngest person to complete the 4 Deserts Grand Slam, running four 250-kilometer ultra-marathons across the driest (Chile), windiest (China), hottest (Sahara), and coldest (Antarctica) deserts on Earth, carrying in a backpack everything she needed to survive
- Clocked 3253 kilometers in a seventy-seven-day run from the west to east of India (2016)
- Cofounder of Freedom Runners, a social enterprise business employing and training young women in South Africa on women's health issues

———————————

Behind the Question
Samantha is highly conscious that we only have a certain

amount of footsteps in our lifetime. She is mindful of every step, whether big or small, and how each step can lead to change for others around the world. As a social impact entrepreneur, author, and speaker, Samantha has set out to make her footsteps count. Sam started running as a break from studying law, but it quickly turned into a journey leading to her running over 20,000 kilometers across every continent. She realized that long-distance running could be her vehicle to serve a higher purpose: advocating for women's empowerment, social change, and access to education.

Samantha enjoys the physical and mental challenges of running, but it's the attention that long-distance running and record-breaking physical feats are able to bring to important causes that motivates her most. As an example, she was able to leverage the media coverage attached to a seventy-seven-day run from west to east India and bring attention to the limited access to quality education in India for children.

We can all have our vehicle to create change, make progress, and ultimately live a life enriched with meaning and purpose. We all have passions, causes, people, and topics that truly light us up. It's about finding the ways to attach meaning to our work (professionally and personally) using a vehicle that personally aligns with our lives. For Samantha, this happens to be creating change through social impact using her vehicle of running.

What is my vehicle to serve a higher purpose?

My vehicle is my podcast *Behind The Human*, unpacking the stories, practices, and questions shaping the lives of extraordinary people. I love having these conversations, but even more so, I love witnessing the impact they have around the world. The show ranks within the top 100 in several countries around the world, which means people are listening, learning, and hopefully finding that one story, practice, or prompt to enrich their lives. This lights me up. Since starting the show, I have been fortunate to host others and use my vehicle to serve a higher purpose.

Before getting to your vehicle, understand what brings meaning and passion to your life. Reflect on the activities, people, and situations that bring a smile to your face. By paying attention to the articles, podcast episodes, and nonfiction books that pique your curiosity, you can take these as signs leading to the causes that mean something to you.

Initially, Samantha found her vehicle to release daily work stress by lacing up her running shoes. Think of the activities serving the same purpose for you right now. Look for what puts you into a flow state—time passing without you noticing and leaving you feeling alive, energized, and motivated. The vehicle also does not have to link to your daily work directly. This notion is often a block for people but does not have to be. While working as a lawyer, Sam ran 379 kilometers nonstop across Australia's Simpson Desert and raised $33,000 for Save the Children Australia. Often, your passion can turn into your future work—exactly what happened to Sam when she left a career in law and was able to support herself through projects related to running. This is not a steadfast rule, so please don't let it block you from starting.

How can I boost my mental enjoyment?

Something strange happens when we dedicate our effort to something that we are incredibly passionate about—we go all in. It can be great for focus and output, but we can also lose sight of everything else around us.

Sam runs races that most of us can't even comprehend. She's at the top of her game and trains at elite levels. Yet, she still goes off course at times, a kilometer off the path to find a nice view for her and her team while they rest. Learning and prioritizing how to sidestep or go off the beaten path for our *mental enjoyment* will also support our performance. Sam has seen this play out time and again, "I guarantee your physical performance flourishes every time you do that."

I remember first embracing the "sidestep" when I was a corporate brand manager. Travelling around the world for conferences and meetings was a requirement. This is the point where I can hear your internal voice saying, "Poor you for travelling around the world. That sounds so challenging." I get it and would make the same judgement, but although I am forever grateful for the opportunity to travel, what most people do not realize is that your work often doubles or triples in these situations. When travelling, you have to be "on" all day and usually into the evening, while also managing communication and tasks happening back home. I started realizing that the locations I was travelling to meant nothing other than a long flight and a hotel room because I wasn't able to experience anything outside of my work, until I decided to sidestep for my own mental enjoyment.

I was tired of busting my ass each day to only look forward to the next vacation where I could truly disconnect. Yet, what if I could inject micro vacation moments weekly and during my work travels? I did just that, and it changed everything. When travelling for work instead of rushing into an Uber and hammering out a few last email replies, I would take that time to walk to my meetings while being present and experiencing my surroundings. The emails could wait. Here's the thing, often when I'd let some time pass, the people on the other side of those emails would figure things out themselves—saving me the replies altogether!

If Sam can make time in a *race* to sidestep off the path and take in the present moment from a beautiful view, so can we.

How can I put my best foot forward?

Some footsteps are for planning, some are for nurturing, some are for reflection. Remember, Sam is conscious of each footstep she takes. Many steps are taken during the race, but often even more steps are taken before and after the event. There is Sam during a project and Sam after a project. She is completely absorbed in the details of a project but is the first to say, "If you don't look after yourself, you can't look after the project." This leads to Sam post-project: ensuring relationships are nurtured, understanding her patterns of behavior during highs and lows, and reflecting on what worked and where she could have been better. These reflective practices allow Sam to operate at her best and continually expand what her best looks like.

You may resonate with the cycle approach or be more inclined to inject more of the post-project practices into the entire experience. Follow what works best and feels right for you. Sam notes, "You can't neglect reflection," so take the time to review individual projects, or chapters of your life, to understand what you learned and where you can grow so that you, too, can expand your definition of you at your best.

Final Thought

Each footstep makes a difference—it's up to us to decide what that difference will be.

How can I heal myself?

John Assaraf

Healed himself of chronic disease, then built
five multimillion-dollar companies

QUICK BIO

- Philanthropist, speaker, and entrepreneur that has built five multimillion-dollar companies
- Globally recognized mindset and performance expert
- Wrote two *New York Times* best-selling books
- Featured in eight movies, including the blockbuster hit *The Secret* and *Quest For Success* with Richard Branson and the Dalai Lama
- Founder and CEO of NeuroGym, a company dedicated to using the most advanced technologies and evidence-based brain training methods to help individuals unleash their fullest potential and maximize their results

---

Behind the Question

At the age of twenty-two, John was taking twenty-five medications a day for his ulcerative colitis and had little to no control of his colon. This meant that it did not matter if he was sitting in his car or just finished having sex—if he had a bowel movement coming, there was no stopping it. This is something none of us would ever want to experience, and especially not a twenty-two-year-old just getting started in the world.

Taking daily medications or going through surgery to remove his entire colon and rectum were not options John was prepared to blindly accept. Thankfully he would soon get the first real glimpse into what was possible with the mind, what he could do by changing his internal narrative from being a victim to being in control. The disease that John described as "being victim to" was also the mental unlock to all his future success as a multimillionaire, author, actor, and highly recognized explorer of consciousness.

John came across a group of doctors on TV speaking about the mind-body connection and how we default to only treating and thinking of the symptoms to a problem. The TV episode left John curious and with a desire to understand if this could be a solution to his ulcerative colitis. The research began and he came across an affirmation that changed everything:

"My body and all its organs were created by the infinite intelligence in my subconscious mind. It knows how to heal me. Its wisdom created all my organs, tissues, bones, and muscles. This infinite healing presence within me is now transforming every atom of my being, making me whole and perfect." —Joseph Murphy

He read this affirmation daily, then closed his eyes and visualized his colon healing. He changed his diet, started exercising, and did everything he could to reduce his stress. Within five weeks of the practice, he completely healed his ulcerative colitis and has never had it since. He has gone on to help a countless number of people unlock their minds to heal.

John wondered if the practice that reversed over two years' of suffering in five weeks could be applied to other areas of life like his career, relationships, or earning money. The answer was yes. John knew that one key step had to take place to make this happen: shifting his frame of mind from thinking he was the victim of his circumstance to taking ownership and control. He has done so in all areas of his life and never looked back.

Where are you playing the victim?

The practice John used to heal himself could not have been realized without first releasing the internal narrative he had around being the victim of a disease. We can also think of this narrative and thoughts as limiting beliefs. We all have them and they show up in all areas of life, but as we saw through John's example, we can choose to release these beliefs.

"You don't have to be a victim to what's happening out there."
—John Assaraf

Where are you playing the victim? It's time to be brutally honest with yourself because playing the victim does nothing for you besides leading you further down the same path and attracting more of what you don't want in your life. How you speak and think (internally and externally) dictates what shows up in your life.

Think of your health, relationships, career, and personal life. Where are you being held back? We can change this. As John says, "Our brains are the most powerful computer in the world," we just need to learn how to operate them. The first step is understanding where we are playing the victim because often we don't even realize this is happening. The following language can help identify where this might be happening:

- "I just wish I could..."
- "I can't..."
- "I'll never be..."
- "I can never..."
- "If only I could..."

A considerable weight lifts off our shoulders when we can shift from victim speak to an affirmative tone of being in control of how we choose to react to situations. It starts with the narrative and words we tell ourselves and leads to the actions we then take. One of the best ways to shift your inner dialogue is through the questions you reflect on. As John has seen time and again, "the power of our questions determine our focus and emotions." He uses questions that empower and lift him up. For example, rephrasing "I can't" to "How can I?" Or, putting "imagine if" in front of your statements.

Just using the word "imagine" immediately puts our mind in a different place, one where rules no longer exist. For example: "Imagine if my bills were covered each month. Imagine if I were in the relationship of my dreams. Imagine if I were stress free." After making *imagine statements* our minds instantly go to how great we would feel in those circumstances, and that starts new internal programming. For more on the imagine mindset and mental fitness, flip to Naveen Jain's profile.

Simple tweaks in language can unlock mindset shifts and abolish the victim speech. Return to the areas where you self-identified as the victim, and spend time in reflection with

"How can I?" in front of the situation. Try not to edit your thoughts. Instead, let them flow freely onto the page. We have the answers to all of our biggest questions when we ask the right questions. Questions propel us forward.

How do I want to design my life?

With the weight of living in victim mode lifted, you can now unleash opportunity and the life you desire. It's not only possible, but something you owe to yourself! With no restrictions, limitations, or boundaries, write down the life you want to live. Write every single detail, from how you want to feel waking up each morning to how you want to feel when your head hits the pillow at night.

When John goes through this exercise, he focuses on return on energy (ROE) and return on investment (ROI). This ensures the activities supporting the life he wants hit on both ROE and ROI. It's a winning combination. You will naturally avoid energy-sucking activities, relationships, and events while putting your focus on the things bringing you the income you require for the life you desire. I realize this may sound overly simplistic, and I'm not saying the journey will be without challenge, but starting with clarity in what you want for your life and the activities to support it will always push you closer to achieving your goals.

John was left with three critical prompts from his first mentor and coach, Alan Brown, who first introduced him to the idea of designing his life. Now I leave them with you:

- What specifically do you want to achieve?
- Why must you achieve these goals?

- Are you interested in, or are you committed to, achieving these goals and living the life of your dreams?

Take the time that feels right for you to reflect on the prompts in this profile. They are big questions to consider. After you've spent time with them, life will never be the same, and you'll crave more prompts to propel you forward. It's exciting, energizing, and rewarding to live life from this perspective. Enjoy the process and the journey!

Final Thought

We can heal and propel forward in life or be a victim. We can't be both.

How can I raise the standard?

Florence Nightingale

Pioneer of modern nursing

May 12, 1820 – August 13, 1910

QUICK BIO

- Internationally-recognized nurse who transformed nursing into a respected profession
- Pioneered global change around proper medical care during the nineteenth and twentieth centuries
- Known for making her rounds in the evening to care for the sick, which gave rise to her image as the The Lady with the Lamp
- Continued to create change from her writing and letters to aid in policy reform despite being bedridden from disease until her eventual death
- A mathematical and statistical genius credited for developing the polar area diagram, a specific form of the traditional pie chart
- First female member of the Royal Statistical Society (1859)
- Despite being globally recognized and her photo being displayed on a bank note by the Bank of England from 1975 until 1994, she was a quiet and reserved person

Behind the Question

The world of healthcare in the 1800's was barely a step up from butchery and torture. Florence Nightingale tolerated these abysmal standards of her era well into her twenties, but there was a lot that she did not accept. As she continued in her career, it became more and more apparent to her that many standards were archaic or outright unjust. These include:

- She did not accept that higher education was only reserved for men
- She did not accept that she was expected to find a husband to support her and never work herself; Florence refused two marriage proposals to avoid being distracted from her work
- She did not accept the low standard of care and unsanitary conditions for patients in a British base hospital
- She did not accept that nursing as a profession was barely considered above prostitution

Because Florence Nightingale did not accept the standards of her time, we have one of the most critical elements of our global healthcare system: a respected nursing profession. She brought respect to nursing and sparked global healthcare reform. Hospitals, doctors, and policymakers could no longer look the other way after Florence was able to cut the death rate of patients by two-thirds in a Crimea British base hospital.

When Florence arrived at the Crimea hospital, the conditions were far from her belief that "the very first requirement in a hospital is that it should do the sick no harm." The hospital was built on top of a sewer, which was flooding the hospital's water supply. There were accounts of patients having to walk through ankle-deep sewage on their way to the washroom. The beds and linens were dirty, and seeing exposed rotting meat was not uncommon. Florence called the hospital the "Kingdom of Hell."

As appalling as the situation was, she was still met with resistance when trying to make changes. Thankfully, Florence was able to rely on her mathematical background to show that 4,000 people had died from war-related injuries in this particular hospital, but 19,000 were killed *because* of the hospital. When Florence returned home, as her biographers have stated, she "...tirelessly devoted her life to preventing disease and ensuring safe and compassionate treatment for the poor and the suffering." After implementing basics like providing clean drinking water, fresh air, and clean linens and bandages to patients, the death rate went from 40% to 2.2%.

The examples are extreme but essential to provide the contrast needed to force a pause, to take a moment for us to reflect on what we may be accepting by default. It's up to us, individually, to first decide which standards we are willing to accept, starting with your internal standards:

- The way you treat yourself
- The way you speak to yourself
- The way you see yourself in this world

Let's raise our bar because we deserve it and are awesome! When we are confident (not cocky), passionate, and internally driven, we can achieve tremendous results.

Naveen Jain (see his profile in part three) once told me that solving billion-person challenges starts with becoming internally clear and dedicating all our energy. When we are clear, and 100 percent behind solving a huge problem, the smartest people in the world will want to join that mission. What Florence Nightingale was able to achieve is a perfect example to prove Naveen's point. To create a global change in nursing and improve the standard of care required support by many. She had the numbers to first shock individuals, but her conviction and dedication to the cause brought along others to create the change we benefit from today.

No matter the size of the challenge, we have to start somewhere. We have to take the first step. As Florence has said, "So never lose an opportunity of urging a practical beginning, however small, for it is wonderful how often in such matters the mustard-seed germinates and roots itself." Spend some time getting clear with the opening prompt, take that first step, and enjoy the journey that unfolds.

What makes me unique?

Well, you are unique because you are you! That's a given. I'm speaking about the different skills and experiences you have picked up along the ride of life and how they can help push your cause forward.

There is no doubt that Florence Nightingale's mathematical skills helped bring attention to the healthcare challenges she was working on solving: she invented the polar area diagram! Who knows where we would be today or what would have come of the healthcare system and nursing profession if she did not leverage her skills to visualize the challenges at hand. Florence clearly used her skills to create change. What matters most is that we unpack our unique abilities to support the actions required to change what we no longer view as acceptable.

Time to write. Get the challenge you are striving to solve out of your head and in front of your eyes. Next, list everything that makes you, you—your character traits, skills, and passions. Try to keep everything in a single view.

Here you are. You have already taken that first step and brought awareness to the situation. Now circle everything on the page that can help support the change you are seeking. For example, if I were trying to bring awareness to something important to me, could I leverage my skills as a podcast host to do so? Could I leverage the fact that I'm a thirty-six-year-old with a full head of natural grey hair in any visuals to help stand out? I know I'm reaching, but something has to come of this hair situation of mine! All to say: get creative.

Florence Nightingale was a woman who became globally known as The Lady with the Lamp, but who also wanted nothing to do with being in the public spotlight, which clearly can be felt from her claim, "I only want to be forgotten." If she had lived in the Instagram era, I suspect she would not be addicted to posting on her feed and certainly would not be chasing the "likes." However, I do imagine she would leverage internet fame to gain access to the people who could help her create change. In fact, in 1860 she leveraged the media of her time and the $250,000 gifted to her by Queen Victoria to open the Nightingale Training School for Nurses at St.Thomas Hospital.

Take a minute to list the connections in your own life that could make things happen. The combination of your unique skill set and those connections can be the very formula required to fuel your cause. We have so much we can leverage, but those connection points and the people who can help us are often buried in our minds until we spend time pulling them out onto the page.

How do I navigate the roadblocks?

I would be remiss to not mention the struggle, roadblocks, and challenges that Florence had to overcome. After begging her parents for thirteen years to become a nurse, finally at the age of thirty she started working in her profession. However, just eight years later she contracted what was known as Crimean fever, leaving her often bedridden and confined to her home for the rest of her life. Remember, she lived until the age of ninety; that's a long time to be living with chronic disease and navigating mental health challenges. Some mood disorder experts concluded it to be bipolar disorder, which could explain why she had thoughts like this: "In my thirty-first year, I can see nothing desirable but death."

I do not present this information to take away from her remarkable contributions to the world, but to share the other side of her story and show that she, too, was human and had to work through her own internal challenges. According to biographer Mark Bostridge, "She should be remembered for the far-sighted reforms that have influenced an entire profession." While confined to her bed, she continued to work and write. She wrote letters to change policy and completed *Notes on Nursing*, a textbook still used today when training to be a nurse.

I think we can agree that it would have been easy for her to stop making efforts and let others continue the legacy, but Florence's mission, purpose, and passion to *not* accept the standards of the time were strong. She reminds me a lot of Stephen

Hawking, someone who could have easily stopped pushing forward due to roadblocks in his health but kept going and did not let limiting beliefs slow him down.

My point is to ensure we are clear in answering the opening prompt because it is through the passion and motivation surrounding your answer that you will navigate through the roadblocks. We can do our best to plan and mitigate risk, but life will happen, and the unexpected will present itself. In these moments, we have the opportunity to choose. As we have seen with Florence Nightingale, global change and a lasting legacy are possible if we decide to continue and fight for our cause.

Final Thought

All it takes is one person to raise the standard. You can be that person.

How can I raise the standard?

Whom haven't I thanked lately?

Chris Schembra

One of the most sought-after dinner hosts in the world—the gratitude guru

QUICK BIO

- Has sparked over 500,000 relationships around the dinner table
- Best-selling author of *Gratitude and Pasta: The Secret Sauce for Human Connection*, chronicling his adventures as one of the most sought-after dinner hosts in the world
- *Forbes* ranks *Gratitude and Pasta* as the number two book of 2020 to create human connection, *USA Today* calls him the Gratitude Guru, and *Inc.* magazine has named him one of their "Icons and Innovators"
- Founding member of the Rolling Stone Culture Council
- Founder and Chief Question Asker of 7:47, an advisory firm which helps companies give the gift of community and belonging to their VIP clients and partners
- Led social campaigns with over one million participants, lowering the suicide rate among veterans with PTSD
- The projects Chris has been involved in have been awarded fourteen Tony Awards, seven Emmy Awards, and a Grammy Award

Behind the Question

In case you haven't noticed yet, I love questions, specifically the power that one question can have. The full version of the opening prompt is: If you could give credit or thanks to one person in your life whom you don't give enough credit or thanks to, whom would that be? This one prompt has sparked over 500,000 relationships around the dinner table, conversations and connections that may have never formed, and internal conversations and reflections with oneself.

Chris has created an entire business (7:47) and movement around this one question—and it started with pasta sauce! Despite a successful career producing and working on projects associated with numerous awards, Chris felt isolated and disconnected from his work. Something was missing: meaningful human connections. After spending time in Italy, immersed in culture and cuisine, he returned to New York City, energized and passionate to experiment in his own kitchen. The result was a delicious pasta sauce that his dinner guests loved! Yet they seemed to enjoy something even more than the sauce— the structure and human connection resulting from the dinner:

> *"Since the inception, the dinner has been the same format: 6:30 pm cocktails, 8:00 pm dinner, but at 7:47 pm, we delegate 11 specific tasks empowering the attendees to be part of the setup process. At 8:30 pm we tell a joke, and at 8:35 pm we open up the table for communal discussion on a specific topic - if you could give credit or thanks to one person in your life [whom] you don't give enough credit or thanks to, [whom] would that be?*

*During that communal discussion piece because we've spent
2 hours already helping people connect, people get vulnerable, open up, and share intimate emotions from their life.*

The tipping point occurred at 2 am on a Monday in February of 2016. Chris woke up in tears, realizing for the first time in his life that he had found complete joy and was starting to rid himself of insecurity. His greatest insecurity in life had been feeling like he was always left out of the group, the last one called to the party." —7:47 Club

Now, Chris was the one bringing the group together and the first one to the party, but he is doing so much more. He is able to stimulate deep personal reflection and gratitude in a matter of minutes. Having participated in one of Chris's virtual gratitude dinners (a COVID pivot), we all were able to share, reflect, and be vulnerable while we dined over pasta together on video chat.

We opened with the same prompt from this profile and immediately started to connect. I did not know anyone in the discussion besides Chris, but we were all there because we trusted his process, and I believe we were all seeking human connection—especially during a time where the pandemic took away so much of that. In a way, we are moving faster than ever to keep up with our responsibilities, but as Chris originally realized from his time in Italy, it's okay to slow down, connect, reflect, and enjoy a meal together.

What relationships do I value most in my life?

The people we choose to surround ourselves with end up forming the person we are or whom we strive to be. We have all heard some rendition of this concept: "You are the average of the five people you spend the most time with." If this is the case, we should probably pick those people wisely and nurture those relationships. It's easy to take relationships for granted. Life moves fast and we all have things to do, but let's not forget the people who helped get us to the very things we are working on.

Even for Chris, the gratitude guru, it's something he's had to work on. "I'd say I suck at showing gratitude to people. I'm only good at it because I've made it my life." We can all make gratitude a part of our lives. Chris sparks gratitude-themed dinners all around the world using one prompt to start the conversation, and so can we!

Bring a few of your most cherished friends together for dinner. Let them know you want to try something different based on what you read here, or through Chris's work, so their minds are primed to be open when they arrive. Then go for it! Ask the question: If you could give credit or thanks to one person in your life whom you don't give enough credit or thanks to, whom would that be?

Having experienced Chris's dinners and having interviewed him, I can guarantee you will not be disappointed in the experience. You might be surprised at what you hear from your guests, and even more so what you hear from yourself.

I have another gratitude system that is easy to keep up which allows me to also nourish a large-scale network. I am often asked how I stay connected with my network, especially with all the people I've been fortunate to interview over the years. The answer is quite simple—I speak with them and express gratitude.

Whenever I think about someone, resonate with one of their

social media posts, or find them passing through my mind, I pause. Then, I send them a text or direct message simply saying something like, "I was just thinking about you and wanted to wish you an awesome day." That's it. It takes seconds but can last a lifetime. The key is to send the message as soon as the person comes to mind. I literally just messaged Chris Schembra between this sentence and the last, expressing my gratitude for him and wishing him a stunning day!

Give it a try. Stop reading, close your eyes, and see who floats into your mind. Don't overthink it, take the first person who appears and send them a short message, whatever feels right and sincere to you. Not only will you make their day with a message that took only seconds for you to write and for them to read, but you'll feel great when they acknowledge your comment. I call this the *gratitude loop*, a loop that never disappoints.

Final Thought

Everyone wins when expressing gratitude.

Whom haven't I thanked lately?

How do I accept the world as it is?

Jerry Colonna
The CEO Whisperer

QUICK BIO

- One of the world's most in-demand executive coaches
- Founder and CEO of Reboot.io, executive coaching and leadership development firm dedicated to the notion that better humans make better leaders
- Author of *Reboot: Leadership and the Art of Growing Up*
- A prior venture capitalist focused on investing in early stage technology-related startups
- Cofounded New York City-based Flatiron Partners with Fred Wilson, which became one of the nation's most successful early-stage investment programs
- Known for making founders cry, in all the right ways, to live and lead at their best
- Lives in Boulder, Colorado

Behind the Question

Three months after 9/11, Jerry stood on a subway platform in New

York City with a decision to make, the most crucial decision of all. Jerry told me, "I had a choice to either live or die." A quick flash of the faces of his kids passed through his mind giving him the pause needed to make a different decision, a decision that not only saved his life but would save the lives of others down the road through his work.

Professionally speaking, Jerry was at the top of his game. Flatiron Partners was one of the hottest venture capital firms of the dot-com era. He was on the pulse, hanging out with the who's who, and doing very well financially. But inside, things were off. As described by Jerry, "The more I hid from my own experience, the more depressed I became."

Jerry is in a very different place now. In fact, far from the New York City subway platform it's not uncommon to hear someone respond with, "That guy saved my life," when describing how they know Jerry.

His journey to "accepting the world as it is" took time, stillness, and continual work. This place, where true happiness exists in any situation, is available to us all. To get there, we first must go down a path that Jerry likes to call "radical self-inquiry." This is a path to understanding our motivators: why we live the way we do or what we are running to and from. Jerry did a lot of work with therapists and spent time in silence with a journal and in nature.

I do not believe there is a prescription for this type of work. We are all unique. During my darkest and most challenging times, removing myself from the noise of life and sitting down with a journal has helped me process the toughest and the greatest situations. That works for me, but you have to find what works for you and it may take some experimentation. Be kind to yourself as you go through the process, and know it will always be worth it in the end.

Spending time quieting your mind on a long walk with only the sounds, sights, and smells of the environment you are in can go a long way, and at the very least it is a great starting point. Spending time in radical self-inquiry is essential because we have years' worth of belief systems to unpack. These belief systems may have once served us but are either no longer doing so or are holding us back. Going through this examination allows for progressive prompts like: Whom do I want to be?

Jerry's inspired reflection can be a lot to consider all at once. I suggest you take your time, be kind to yourself, and chip away at what has built up over the years in order to reveal your most authentic self. I have gone through this process myself and continue to work on meeting the world as it is. As you can imagine, it takes work and time. There is a lightness in the air when operating from this perspective. Not to say each day feels marvelous, but the more I implement and experiment with the practices outlined in this book, the more frequently I tap into this lightness. And it feels damn good!

What is impermanent in your life?

Okay—this is a trick question, because *everything* is impermanent. We often forget this fact. Everything that we love will end, but everything we despise will end as well. Those thoughts of self-doubt, fear, anxiety, and uncertainty will end. The same rule applies to the feeling of success when shipping a project, getting that promotion, publishing your first book (had to include this one), or seeing your podcast hit the top fifty list—all impermanent. These are all quick hits of dopamine that will pass versus the daily satisfaction of finding joy in the process itself.

Jerry shared a shocking example on the podcast with me to illustrate the point: Tibetan sand mandalas. If you want to go down a YouTube rabbit hole, Google this stuff. The colors and detail of these sand mandalas are stunning. Sand mandalas are meticulously created using different colored sand trickling out of a small pipe to create a masterpiece. Often taking days to create, and once completed, the work of art is destroyed. That's right, no selfies with the sand mandala. It's gone, which is precisely the point. The tradition takes place to symbolize the impermanence of the situation and emotion.

When the concept of impermanence sets in, life just gets better by default. We are happier. We attract more happiness in our life; people, opportunities, and wonderful experiences show up more frequently. That lightness to life I described earlier becomes the default, and again, that's freaking awesome.

Much of what has been discussed in this profile leads back, in some way, to the present moment. I believe this is one of the most incredible superpowers we can tap into. Being present, fully engaged, like a monk creating a sand mandala, typically pauses any other narrative running through your mind. With a little training, we can be present and fully engaged with absolutely anything.

The more we train our minds with practices like journaling, meditation, and mindfulness walks, the more we can access the present moment on command or naturally as we enter various situations. These practices help our minds acknowledge thoughts, release them, and allow us to focus on the moment in front of us.

Journaling is one of those practices Jerry leverages. "I journal for the moment-to-moment experience of being fully present in whatever it is I am feeling." Try out Jerry's approach, what many would call freewriting, or what Julia Cameron, author of *The Artist's Way*, would describe as "morning pages—three pages of longhand, stream of consciousness writing, done first thing in the morning."

As mentioned at the beginning of the profile, we all have the opportunity to accept our circumstances and the world as it is. Jerry has left us with many beautiful prompts and methods to shift our perspective and help us along the journey of accepting what is.

Final Thought

Release the mental weight of permanence; all is impermanent.

How do I accept the world as it is?

How am I finding my way?

Shantell Martin
World-renowned visual artist

QUICK BIO

- Artist and cultural facilitator, forging new connections between fine art, education, design, philosophy, and technology
- Her work is a meditative process defined by an uninhibited flow and embodiment of her internal state and the impermanence of the world around her
- Artwork has appeared in the Brooklyn Museum, Museum of Contemporary African Diasporan Arts, Bata Shoe Museum, and a number of private galleries
- Collaborated with artists such as Pulitzer Prize-winning performance artist Kendrick Lamar and acclaimed designer Kelly Wearstler
- Former adjunct professor and Artist In Residence at NYU's Interactive Telecommunications Program (ITP, a two-year graduate program located in the Tisch School of the Arts) and MIT Media Lab Visiting Scholar
- Born in London and attended Central St. Martins University

Behind the Question

As I write this, I have interviewed over 200 top performers about their mental fitness practices. Each interview starts with the same question: Who are you? I have come to realize it's a risky question because it's deep and requires someone to think about their life in real time while potentially answering a question they may never have thought about. I promise, I'm not an asshole. There is a reason for this prompt!

For the podcast, I simply ask the question to avoid receiving a job title as the main descriptor for that person's life. We often default to *what we do* to define *who we are*. We are more than just a job title, we are stunning humans with values, skills, and unique characteristics. Behind the human is where the magic lives.

However, I do have a hidden agenda with the question, one I have never shared before. My hidden desire is to stimulate personal reflection outside of the interview for the guest. By asking a loaded question to begin my interviews, I can only expect an intuitive answer in the moment unless they have already given the prompt some thought. It is my hope that by the end of our interview, they leave more curious about themselves than they had been before coming into the conversation. I have the same desire with the conversation we are having together through this book. For the record, 99% of guests laugh and say something like, "Wow, we're starting things off light," and then we have a beautiful conversation.

Shantell was part of the 99%, but she provided a unique twist to the situation. She answered the question with a question—my kind of human! After explaining how many of us struggle in finding the vocabulary to answer a question like "Who are you?" she provided a more practical question to kick things off: How are you finding your way? I love how the prompt reframes and lightens the reflection while still allowing us to get truly honest with ourselves. Shantell's answer to her own question:

"I'm finding my way in life through this language of words, lines, drawings, characters, and faces which help create connections and experiences." —Shantell Martin

It's important we give ourselves time and self-love throughout the process. Before Shantell could find her way and begin to understand who she was, she first had to be clear in who she was not, which allowed her to foster confidence and be able to say, "I'm going to do what I'm going to do." Much of who we are not can come from others defining who we are, putting us in boxes built by society; yet we are all our own person with unique qualities and desires.

This is a good place to pause and think. Understand how you have been finding your way through life and how much of that path has been dictated by others. There may be alignment in how others see you and how you see yourself, which is fantastic, but it does not hurt to check back in and make sure this is still the case.

When speaking of the great artists before her time, Shantell realized, "They are all these old dead white guys that you can't see yourself in," and then she was told, "You can't do what they're doing." She did not accept this, but instead leaned in and left me with, "My life came about having security and confidence in myself." After spending time getting clear, Shantell was able to fully lean in and live out her life with intention.

Where can I lean in?

Shantell described a time when she was in front of a couple hundred people for a museum show at MoCADA (Museum of Contemporary African Diasporan Arts) and was too scared to turn around. However, when she did turn and wave to the audience, who were eagerly waiting for her pen to touch the canvas, they all waved back in unison. She had leaned into the experience and realized, "We were all connected through these lines I was making."

From that point forward, nothing else mattered but harnessing the energy from the crowd and letting her pen do whatever it needed to do. The fear was gone, and Shantell realized that by fully leaning into the moment she didn't have the time to be anyone else but herself. In her words, "I don't have time to be insecure or overthink things or be distracted."

I can't help but feel refreshed recounting this story. Moving from fear to being completely dialed into her art, audience, and energy, Shantell became her authentic self. It's refreshing and encouraging because we all have our version of Shantell's pen. For me, it's leaning in, fully present, behind the podcast mic in order to connect and exchange energy with each guest no matter how big or small their influence may be. They are human, and we are doing a human thing: having a conversation.

I received a compliment from Pulitzer Prize-nominated and New York Times best-selling author Steven Kotler after I thanked him for his time on the show. He turned the gratitude back to me by saying, "Thank you for your energy. I could not do this each day without it." His comment lit me up for days in the same way a unified wave from the MoCADA crowd energized

Shantell to fully lean in and create. Think about where you can lean in. What energy exchange do you want to take place, and with whom?

> *"I am so fortunate that I draw as a career,*
> *or as a hobby or as everything in between, because it means*
> *I'm constantly using this tool, that is a meditation in a way,*
> *and does allow me to pause and does allow me to reflect*
> *and does keep me present." —Shantell Martin*

Is my white space expanding?

When we get clear about who we want to be and fully lean into that person, craft, and energy, a heightened level of confidence and a honing of our craft follows. I asked Shantell what she noticed has changed or evolved over the years with her art. She had a beautiful response, "The main change is the white space is growing. The nothingness is growing." Then after providing her answer, she wondered, "What am I leaving behind?" The magic and evolution lives in reflecting on that prompt in order to understand how you are evolving, what that means, and how you can leverage the understanding as you move forward.

I have noticed that I ask far fewer questions in an interview, but that the questions I do ask are much more intentional, personalized, and impactful. The same is true in the questions I ask myself during my personal reflection.

> *"I do feel there is a confidence in being able to put one*
> *line on a whole canvas and walk away. And perhaps*
> *that's what I'm walking towards." —Shantell Martin*

Take a pause, sit in silence, and think about what you have walked away from on your journey and what you are walking towards. Whatever your "one line on a canvas" may be, make sure to show up proud, lean in, and enjoy the journey!

Final Thought

We all have access to a blank canvas—draw your first line today.

PART THREE

Expand
Possibility

Attaining a state of expanded possibility opens up an incredible space to us. It's a place where anything is possible, where things just happen. The right people show up and unimaginable ideas and opportunities surface.

It is no accident that people like Steve Jobs, Maya Angelou, and Naveen Jain could see into the future and beyond what was possible in the present moment. Through their clarity, monomaniacal focus, and intentionality, they could expand possibility not only for themselves but also for countless others.

And yes, so can we, by upgrading the questions guiding us at this phase of our journey. The questions may look similar, but the meaning behind them is world class. Hold on, and enjoy the ride.

How do I rise up?

Maya Angelou
American poet, memoirist, and civil rights activist

April 4, 1928 – May 28, 2014

QUICK BIO

- Maya Angelou (born Marguerite Annie Johnson) was an American author, actress, screenwriter, dancer, poet, and civil rights activist
- She stopped speaking completely for five years after being raped by her mother's boyfriend when she was just eight years old
- Her early life was the focus of her 1969 memoir, *I Know Why the Caged Bird Sings,* making literary history as the first nonfiction bestseller by an African American woman
- Received several honors including two NAACP Image Awards in Outstanding Literary Work for Nonfiction in 2005 and 2009
- Awarded the Presidential Medal of Freedom in 2011

Behind the Question

Maya Angelou is known for the words she spoke. Her words inspired stories that led to movements and helped people feel worthy, seen, and loved. She's published seven autobiographies, three books of essays, and an abundance of poetry. And, for five years, she never spoke a single word.

Maya experienced something no person should have to, a violent rape at the age of eight years old. Reluctantly, she ended up telling her brother, leading to other family members finding out, and, ultimately, the rapist was found dead a day after being released from prison. Maya literally stopped speaking for five years because she thought her words had killed a man.

Despite living in silence, Maya found the silver lining to a horrific experience. She read nonstop. She read everything. She memorized poetry. She consumed every book in the black school library and anything she could get her hands on from the white school library.

"When I decided to speak, I had a lot to say and many ways in which to say what I had to say." —Maya Angelou

It was Mrs. Bertha Flowers, described by Maya as the aristocrat of Black Stamps, who ended her silence. In *I Know Why the Caged Bird Sings*, Maya says "She was one of the few gentlewomen I have ever known, and has remained throughout my life the measure of what a human being can be." It was Mrs. Flowers who would read poetry to Maya and asked her to consume all the literature in the library, but it was also she who said, "You'll never love poetry until you feel it come out of your mouth." This bothered Maya because although she adored poetry and respected Mrs. Flowers, she still did not want to speak.

Mrs. Flowers was relentless, chasing and harassing Maya until finally, after five years' of silence, Maya went under her house and recited a poem aloud, coming to the realization, "I had left my voice, my voice hadn't left me." At that moment, she rose from her trauma—and never stopped rising.

> *You may shoot me with your words,*
> *You may cut me with your eyes,*
> *You may kill me with your hatefulness,*
> *But still, like air, I'll rise.*
> —*excerpt from* Still I Rise *by Maya Angelou*

Irrespective of what we want to rise up from, we have to make the decision on our own. People, circumstances, and experiences can all help, but ultimately, as Maya chose to break her silence by reciting a poem, we have to take that first step as well. We all deserve to rise up, flourish, and not be silenced.

Where do I find the courage to rise up?

We could be choosing to rise up in many situations, but there is one thing required for them all—courage. Whether that be the courage to take the first step in prioritizing our health or be the courage to set foot on stage to speak in front of an audience, courage is the unlock. Maya used a practical mental hack to tap into courage at a moment's notice:

> *"One of the things I do when I step up on a stage, when I stand up to translate, when I go to teach my classes, when I go to direct a movie, I bring everyone who has ever been kind to me with me—Black, White, Asian, Spanish-speaking, Native American, gay, straight, everybody. I say, 'Come with me. I'm going on the stage, come with me, I need you now.' You see? So I don't ever feel I have no help."* —*Maya Angelou*

We all have those people who have been kind to us, but we rarely think about who they are. Let's do that now. List those people in your life who have been kind, respectful, and inspirational. List those who provide the courage needed to rise up.

In book one of *Meditations* by Marcus Aurelius, he does this very thing. He lists and describes all the people in his life who have expanded his mind, touched his heart, and guided him through experiences. For some, he wrote a few paragraphs; and for others, such as his adoptive father Roman emperor Antoninus Pius, he wrote several pages.

This exercise also doubles as an excellent gratitude practice for the people who mean the most to you. Do not spare any detail. The more you describe, the easier it will be to recall the people and characteristics you admire when you need them most. We can also leverage the same people, or others depending on the situation, to help us work through challenging conditions. Maya would consider what her grandmother's actions and words would be, "Now what would grandma do? What would she say?" Sometimes a subtle shift in perspective is all that is required to unlock the answers we seek.

> *"If you don't like a situation you try to change it. Do whatever you can to change it. And if everything you do falls flat, and you can't change it, then change the way you think about it."* —Maya Angelou

How do I help others rise up?

There is no doubt Maya Angelou found the courage she needed to rise up. She rose up into her mid-eighties, leaving behind a legacy that still inspires us today. It is no accident that Maya serves as a mentor and role model years after her passing. She was intentional in being there for others.

> *"I've had so many rainbows in my clouds...prepare yourself*
> *so that you can be a rainbow in somebody else's cloud."*
> —*Maya Angelou*

How would you like people to speak and think of you when you are not in the room? What characteristics make you, you? Can you be that rainbow in somebody else's cloud? All it takes is a decision to show up each day as the person you want to be remembered for. Write down how you want to show up for others, or stick a note somewhere that will serve as your daily reminder.

During Maya's funeral, Oprah Winfrey shared, "Her great gift to us is that she made us feel heard and seen and loved and worthy. You alone are enough, she taught me." Let us never forget the people who give us courage, help us through life, pick us up when we are down, and celebrate when we are up. We are or can be that person for others.

Final Thought

Rise up for yourself to then rise up for others.

How do I rise up?

What if it were possible?

Naveen Jain
Moonshot-thinking billionaire entrepreneur

QUICK BIO

- Entrepreneur and philanthropist driven to solve the world's biggest challenges through innovation
- Founder of several successful companies including Moon Express, Viome Inc., Bluedot, TalentWise Inc., Intelius, and InfoSpace
- Viome is focused on disrupting healthcare with the goal of "making illness elective" by identifying microbial biomarkers that are predictive of chronic diseases and to adjust the microbial imbalance through personalized nutrition
- Moon Express is the only company in the world to have the permission to leave Earth's orbit and land on the moon with the goal to harvest planetary resources and to develop infrastructure to make humanity a multi-planetary society
- Ernst & Young Entrepreneur of the Year, Siliconindia's Most Admired Serial Entrepreneur
- Director of the board at the XPRIZE foundation

Behind the Question
When I think about Naveen Jain, possibility comes to mind.

Not just any possibility or someone playing lip service to it, but someone who truly believes and has taken action through the businesses he has created. Naveen believes, "Every problem is solvable. It's your mindset that tells you what you can or cannot do."

Only a few short minutes with Naveen leaves you in a realm of possibility that encompasses the wildest thoughts from your imagination. He is a billionaire by default because he sets his mind to solve billion-dollar problems that push humanity forward. While doing so, he stops along the way to help and lift others up.

I will never forget my first meeting with Naveen. One week before our scheduled podcast, Naveen replied to my email within the hour to reconfirm his attendance. He is the billionaire that makes you feel like you are just as important as anything else in his life. Days of research and preparation went by, and I finally found myself behind the mic with one of the most stunning humans on the planet. Then, the unexpected happened. Naveen said, "Marc, we can schedule a podcast at any point; why don't we use this time for you. How can I help you?" I was shocked and immensely grateful for what turned into a thirty-minute business coaching session.

We did end up rescheduling the podcast which you will hear through this profile. Regarding the opening question, there is something magical that sparks in our minds simply by putting two words in front of any sentence: *Imagine if.* When we use the word "imagine," all rules, previous assumptions, and judgements are released. We are free to imagine and paint a picture of possibility without constraints.

Reflecting on the opening prompt primes our mind to shift

into a realm of possibility. By layering on the power of your imagination, just as Naveen does to solve billion-person problems, you are several steps further than anyone else who will just say, "It can't be done, I don't think it's possible, how could we do that...." With a clear picture in your mind of what's possible, your idea can now be shared with others to help solve the challenge together. *This* is how you start solving billion-person challenges and attract smart and motivated humans to sign up for the ride.

What limits am I setting?

To think and live life through the lens of possibility, we have to start by deprogramming any limiting beliefs restraining our imagination. As Naveen says, "We are all born with potential and no limits at all. Society trains us on the limits. This is a learned problem; so if it's learned, we can unlearn." You might be able to think of apparent limiting beliefs like "I don't have the skills or knowledge...," but then there are limiting beliefs we may not be aware of.

For example, we have all heard at some point "The sky's the limit." It is a well-intentioned statement to motivate us to think anything is possible, but there is a flaw in the thinking. Naveen shifted my perspective immediately when disagreeing, "The sky is not the limit. The sky actually doesn't exist—it's a part of our imagination." The point being, we set limits without even realizing we are doing so. How many of these "skies" have we created in our life? Fortunately, given the question nerd that I am, we can navigate and release these limits through questions and curiosity.

Let's take the *sky's the limit* example. One pointed question like "What is the sky?" can completely change your perspective on something that we see daily, but of which we probably have minimal understanding. Just searching the answer will open up another world of discovery and knowledge which will most likely lead to other questions, and ultimately a greater understanding.

Go for it, take one hour this week to reflect on three of the most critical areas of your life, and start asking questions to understand where you have set limits. As an example, let's take a popular association most have with their career and financial health. You have a job that brings in a certain income, either covering your current expenses or not; simple math, but math that also comes with limits. Imagine scenarios that could bring in different revenue streams augmenting your total income outside of a standard job. Leverage Naveen's "imagine language" to think in terms of possibility! The same goes for expenses. Imagine if other people covered your costs. How would that feel, and what would that look like? It may not be happening right now, but it's possible.

As I write this, I have an $8,000 soundproof booth being shipped to my house to take my podcast recording experience to the next level. For years, I've struggled to find a quiet, reliable, and cost-effective recording environment. Now I have one coming, and it did not cost me anything. I took action by emailing every single soundproof booth company and showing them the value of partnering with me and the podcast, which led to the fantastic podcast sponsor (Loop Phone Booths) I now have. One thing is for sure, had I not paused to think and imagine what could be possible, I would not have this booth on the way. A new level of possibility opens up when we remove the limits put in place by us in the first place.

How do I know if this is the right decision?

Much of what has been discussed in this profile will result in new thinking, ideas, and decisions to be made. Whether big or small, Naveen has a process allowing him to reach a clear and certain decision within fifteen minutes. He shuts his eyes and imagines himself six months into the future with the decision made. Spare no detail. See yourself in action doing the things that would result from the decision you are about to make. Visualize every element then ask: How do I feel?

No matter how many spreadsheets or arguments are presented to Naveen surrounding a decision, it all boils down to one thing: how does he feel after the decision has been made? If he feels uneasy or uncomfortable in any way, he walks away. He's walked away from deals that, in the moment, looked incredibly lucrative, but ended up exploding down the road.

When we quiet our minds, we can access an innate and intuitive power available to us all: the ability to see, hear, and feel the signs. When living through the lens of possibility while releasing limiting beliefs and tapping into our innate intuition, we can solve challenges that were once deemed impossible. The bigger the challenge and the more people you can help, the bigger the reward.

Final Thought

Our imagination determines what is possible and what is not.

What if it were possible?

What do we want to know?

Larry King

Broadcasting interview legend

November 19, 1933 – January 23, 2021

QUICK BIO

- Born in Brooklyn, New York, as Lawrence Harvey Zeiger, but changed his name twelve minutes before he went live on air for the first time
- Conducted over 60,000 interviews
- Hosted *Larry King Live* on CNN for over twenty-five years
- His ex-wife suggested he wear suspenders on *Larry King Live* after he had heart surgery and was looking trim.

Behind the Question

"My guest is Frank Sinatra. Why are you here?" With those words, Larry King opened a rare and candid interview with the private singer. He did not pretend Sinatra was his good buddy or make small talk. He led with an honest question, the one question everyone wanted answered. Frank was there because he owed a favor to Jackie Gleason, a well-known comedian and one of Larry's good friends. That favor became a three-hour history-maker. Frank shared parts of his life he had never discussed, including the kidnapping of his son—a detail that Sinatra's publicist had made very clear to Larry that he could not ask about. The topic rose naturally from their honest, connected conversation.

Right after Larry's death, his good friend Cal Fussman released a podcast episode as a final farewell and obituary, noting that Larry "was simply curious why people were the way they were." Larry's genuine curiosity allowed him to get to the truth and uncover what we all wanted to know. His questions captivated audiences for decades, and he built lasting friendships along the way.

Frank Sinatra initially showed up for an interview with Larry because he owed someone a favor, but that first conversation sparked a lifelong friendship. Later in life, when Larry landed in the hospital due to a stroke, Frank Sinatra turned his room into a floral sanctuary with flowers to lift his spirits.

Okay, it's time to apply Larry's interviewing philosophy to our own lives. We can all benefit from slowing down to think about what we genuinely want to understand. You do not have to be a radio or podcast host to leverage the benefits of asking honest and straightforward questions. Larry lived eighty-seven years with over 60,000 interviews to practice this skill, so be kind to yourself when training your mind and crafting your skills. The first time he went on air, it was nearly a disaster (more to come on this), but he persisted and became one of the most well-known broadcasters of all time.

Identify a situation you are faced with right now. You could be interviewing someone for a job, starting a new project, or questioning what's next for your life. Whatever it is, make it personal and pause to ask the opening prompt: What do I want to know? When you answer that question, ask it again. Are you responding with what you *really* want to know? There is no sense staying on the surface with yourself—no judgement. Keep asking the question until you feel honest answers are surfacing.

Am I being honest?

Larry faded the music and prepared to speak on air for the first time. He had dreamed of being a broadcaster ever since he was a little kid pretending to interview players from the Brooklyn Dodgers using rolled up newspapers as his microphone. Now, here he was, the moment he had always dreamed of, the first opportunity to live out his dream—and he couldn't speak.

Larry was human and nervous like any person would be. He had also just been given the name Larry King minutes before going live. The station manager told him his last name Zeiger was too ethnic, and people would have a hard time pronouncing it. With an advertisement for King's Wholesale Liquors in the *Miami Herald* sitting in front of them, Larry's manager turned to him and asked, "How about Larry King?" The unexpected name change did not help calm Larry's nerves going on air for the first time. He froze, but learned a valuable lesson that would shape his interview style up until the final days before passing: Be honest with people.

Being honest sounds obvious, but when we really think about it, we are more dishonest with others and ourselves than we think. I'm not talking about large lies, but moreso the things we do frequently to ever so slightly shift the perception others have of us. Posting the highlights of our life on Instagram is a perfect example. We have all done it, posting that photo of the perfect [name the situation] to show others how incredible things are in our life. I'm being overly dramatic, but take a moment to review what you posted on social media in the last month and ask yourself why you uploaded what you did. Be honest, no bullshit, what was the real motivator?

I'll stop here, because the psychology of social media could be an entire book by itself. My point being, there are many areas in our lives where we are in small ways insincere and could benefit from honesty, as you will see through the rest of this profile.

Okay, back to Larry. Remember, he was frozen behind the mic live on air for the first time, but then he made the decision to be honest with his audience and opened the show: "Good morning, my name is Larry King. I just got that name. I've wanted to be on the radio all my life, and this is my first day, and I'm scared. Please bear with me." By being honest, Larry felt the audience would cut him some slack knowing it was his first time on air. This alone was enough to let the words flow and start a career in broadcasting that would answer the questions everyone else wanted to know.

Let's take a minute to get honest with ourselves. Think about where fear is holding you back from speaking the truth. Write out the details of the situation and how you would feel being totally honest, first with yourself and then with others. Lift the weight off your shoulders and sit in this newfound comfort. As Cal Fussman said, "Larry got people to say what was on their minds by making them comfortable." Use a page of your journal to bring comfort to yourself, and speak your mind. Be honest and free your thoughts and emotions. I imagine it was not comfortable being vulnerable live on air for the first time. Larry could have avoided some of the discomfort by giving technical excuses to justify the dead air. These excuses, though, would serve only to save face and his ego.

I came away with a valuable realization from Larry's interview style. When he was honest and respected himself, guests, and his audience, he could expect the same honesty and respect in return. I wonder if we would have experienced the same level of truth that we came to expect from Larry had he decided to be dishonest that first day on air. I for one, leave inspired by him to ask honest questions, trusting that I will be met with honest answers in return.

Final Thought

Be met with honesty when you show up authentically as yourself.

What do we want to know?

How do I become irreplaceable?

Coco Chanel

Revolutionary stylist and designer of the 1900s

August 19, 1883 – January 10, 1971

QUICK BIO

- Gabrielle Bonheur "Coco" Chanel a french fashion designer, businesswoman, and founder of the Chanel brand
- Revolutionized a fashion era from corseted silhouettes to comfortable, simple, and sophisticated clothing for women
- Known for her trademark Chanel black suit and little black dress
- 100 years later, Chanel N°5 is arguably still one of the most iconic perfumes
- Only fashion designer listed on *Time* magazine's list of the 100 Most Influential People of the 20th Century

---

Behind the Question

As described in the documentary, *Inside Chanel*, Coco seized the present, dared to transform, and created with passion. This formula is at the core of all her work and made her the irreplaceable style icon we know today. Yet as a young girl, I can only imagine she felt nothing further from *irreplaceable*, having been sent to live in an orphanage at just twelve years old after her mother's death. The orphanage was run by nuns dressed in black and white, a color theme that surfaced later in Coco's life when she brought her iconic *little black dress* to the world. A dress that has been described as "simple and accessible to women of all classes" and would become "a sort of uniform for all women of taste."

I cannot say for certain that she sat in silence reflecting on how she could become irreplaceable, but I do know her process and philosophy on life left an irreplaceable legacy. The opening question is designed to stimulate thought around our unique offering and the presence we bring to this world.

Think about how you want people to speak of you when your physical body leaves this earth. How would your eulogy sound and feel to the people celebrating your life? Take time with these prompts and write it out. I know, it sounds dark at first, but reframe the exercise as a celebration of the life you want to live! It's a great way to understand how you want to be remembered. Use this reflection to understand any gaps between your current actions and the presence you want to leave with others.

What presence do I want left behind?

I never personally met Coco, but when I think of someone commanding a presence, I think of her and the brand she created. It's no surprise that the products she brought to this world command that same presence. Listen to her speak about perfume as "the unseen, unforgettable, ultimate accessory of fashion...that heralds your arrival and prolongs your departure." The product description for the timeless and iconic N°5 perfume by Chanel still carries Coco's presence:

> *"N°5, the very essence of femininity. An aldehyde*
> *floral bouquet housed in an iconic bottle with a min-*
> *imalist design. A timeless, legendary fragrance."*

My editor shared her mother's lifelong dream of having a giant bottle of N°5 on display in her home. At first, I did not understand why, but now with Coco's words in my mind, I can see how a simple bottle fuelled by a legendary brand can command an inspiring presence. Imagine leaving behind an iconic legacy like this with your words, actions, and personality. Think of those people in your life who command a presence outlasting their departure. Note the characteristics that stick in your mind and the ones you also have or want to have. Which unique characteristics will prolong your departure? Are they clear to you, and most importantly, are they the characteristics you want to leave with others?

It's totally fine if you do not want to command a Coco Chanel presence, but what Coco's life can teach us is to think about how we want to exist and what we want to leave behind. Whether we consciously think about it or not, our presence is left behind, and I would rather give that some thought. Once we are clear and confident in ourselves, we walk into a room differently. We walk with intention and with a mind primed to see the details that others may not. It's an attitude or mantra to life. As Coco says, "In order to be irreplaceable, one must always be different."

How do I foster legendary confidence?

I believe Coco's confidence level left no room for unwanted mental narratives like self-doubt or fear. Instead, she saw what others could not. In a *Forbes* profile on Coco Chanel, Simon Graj, articulated these points beautifully:

> *"She listened to the world around her and articulated the vision everyone yearned to have. She enabled and facilitated a fashion cyclone that was gestating in the collective soul of her time. We're all witnessing the same events; but, as is usually the case, it takes genius to detect the significance of what's happening.*

> *Coco Chanel had enough confidence in herself to rely on her own judgment. She was famous for saying: 'The most courageous act is still to think for yourself. Aloud.' That goes to the very source of game-changing creativity."*

Coco triggered a ripple effect of opportunity for herself with her ability to "seize beauty all the time, everywhere you go." It was the combination of this presence and unwavering confidence that gave her all she needed to follow her intuition, daring to transform and create.

Time to upgrade your confidence. For the next seven days, before you fall asleep, let's rock some confidence-building visualizations! I often run visualization practices before falling asleep because it's a great way to slow down the mind while also programming a wanted narrative.

Take a few minutes while lying in bed to visualize yourself at your most confident. Use an upcoming situation that could use a boost of confidence, playing out the scene exactly as you want simply by closing your eyes and imagining the experience. Just like an Olympic skier visualizes every detail of their run before they physically do it, you can mentally play out your life before it physically materializes. Close your eyes and feel the experience; your mind will do the rest. With consistent programming and visualization, just like consistent exercise at the gym, the results will appear.

Final Thought

Confidence with presence breeds irreplaceability.

How do I become irreplaceable?

How can I hold space for others?

Claude Silver
First Chief Heart Officer at VaynerMedia

QUICK BIO

- Spent twenty years at Fortune 50 companies guiding client relationships and global brand and advertising strategies
- Created the first-ever Chief Heart Officer (CHO) integrating heart into work at VaynerMedia, a digital agency founded by entrepreneur, best-selling author, and social media guru Gary Vaynerchuk
- Previously worked at VaynerMedia and left to pursue another path before coming back as their CHO
- Life purpose is to be of joyful service and unlock emotional optimism in all
- Maya Angelou's salvo is Claude's North Star: "People will forget what you said, people will forget what you did, but people will never forget how you made them feel"

Behind the Question

When preparing for my interview with Claude, I remember thinking, "She seems like the complete opposite of what I am seeing from someone like Gary Vaynerchuk—who is working nonstop and preaches the benefits of the side hustle. Don't get me wrong, Claude works extremely hard, but there is a different vibe to her, a calming and grounding baseline. In retrospect, I can see why Claude and Gary work so well together; they balance each other out, ultimately providing a winning formula for each employee and client at VaynerMedia.

I was particularly interested in learning how she was able to hold space for hundreds of people across multiple countries. Every call I've ever had with Claude leaves me feeling energized, and I can feel she is 100% present with me. That's just me. Consider all the other conversations she has throughout the day to support the 800 plus employees at VaynerMedia.

I started by being curious about her techniques to hold space for others but grew even more interested in how she was holding space for herself, how she trains her mind to truly be present, listen, and maintain her own energy. We will get to those answers shortly, but first let's set the stage for what it means to hold space for others. Claude defines holding space for others as "being with a person and bearing witness." She describes the idea as being "a vessel for that person to share." She creates a safe and judgement-free environment for the person in front of her. In order to do this, Claude was clear that the first step has to be active listening. That means eliminating distractions, like your phone, or internal stories. It all needs to stop to be present and hold space for another human.

Reflect on how you show up for others. Take care to avoid internal or external distractions, especially if you are holding space for others. Without the internal work or mental fitness, by default, it's nearly impossible to be fully present for another person. This leads us to how Claude holds space for herself in order to hold it for others.

What makes you feel free and limitless?

Claude, just like us, has internal narratives, gets placed in emotionally-charged situations, and has to manage her mind so she can fully show up for others. When Claude feels mentally blocked or feels an unwanted internal narrative developing, she goes inside her mind to experience moments that made her feel grateful, free, and limitless. This exercise helps escape looping narratives and mental blocks. The dopamine and serotonin neurochemical cocktail you'll receive from expressing gratitude will also instantly shift your mood to a happy place.

We are "shaking things up" in our minds to remember we have a lot of awesomeness in our lives. These memories can be used as triggers to reset the mind and blow out the block. This prompt and the energy of feeling free and limitless reminds me of Naveen Jain's use of "imagine" language. When you imagine or think of being free and limitless, all the rules are lifted and anything is possible. It's such a great way to shift perspective, use a new approach, and let go of that internal narrative.

Take time with this prompt, a progressive question, which by default will only shift you forward. From your reflection, make a list of all the experiences, activities, and people that make you feel free and limitless. Keep it close, and the next time your mind needs a reset, consult your list to shift the chemistry in your mind!

How will I protect my energy?

At this point in my conversation with Claude, the answers to my original questions naturally started surfacing around how she could have the energy to hold space for so many people. She has a practical and quick process she calls "energy separations," a practice she picked up years ago when training in chakra healing and energy protection. I paused my visual of lightning bolts beaming from Claude's office windows and employees walking out with smoking hair and was immediately intrigued. To my surprise, no lightning or smoking hair, but instead a straightforward process that we can use to protect our energy.

Claude starts the energy separation immediately following a conversation. Instead of stewing in the words spoken and emotions shared, Claude neutralizes and releases that energy in order to fully show up for the next conversation or activity. The process is super simple and focuses on stating differences to take the force of the energy away.

Here's an example with a fictitious person named Bob:

- I have green eyes, he has blue eyes.
- My name starts with a C, his name starts with a B.
- I have one baby girl, he has three boys.
- I was born in New York City, he was born in Cleveland, Ohio.

Then she gets up, shakes her hands, the purpose being to physically shake out the past energy, and resets to rock the next conversation. I absolutely love the process because in a matter of minutes you can prevent hours, days, weeks, and years of emotional build up.

Final Thought

To hold space for others, first understand how to hold space for yourself.

How do I shift fear to impact?

Daniela Fernandez

Created the world's largest network of entrepreneurs protecting our ocean

QUICK BIO

- Founded the Sustainable Ocean Alliance (SOA) as a college-room idea at Georgetown University when she was nineteen
- SOA has created the world's largest network of young Ocean Leaders in over 150 countries and launched the world's first Ocean Solutions Accelerator
- Recognized for her work by U.S. Secretary John Kerry, U.S. President Bill Clinton, and E.U. Commissioner Karmenu Vella
- Awarded the 2020 Rising Star Visionary Award by the Silicon Valley Forum and named a 2019 *Forbes* 30 Under 30 Social Entrepreneur
- Keynote speaker at The Economist Group's World Ocean Summit, Global Climate Action Summit, the United Nations, the Capitol Hill Ocean Week, the Collision Conference, the Sustainable Brands Conference, WE Day, and Davos 2019 (The World Economic Forum's annual meeting)

Behind the Question

It started with penguins, shuffling around with their densely packed black and white feathers on cold slippery ice sheets in the Arctic. At least that's what Daniela thought the image was supposed to be, but what she was looking at was far from this reality. She saw an image of penguins walking on a sandy beach on a poster advertising Al Gore's documentary *An Inconvenient Truth*. Blown away, left curious, Daniela had to watch the documentary immediately.

In typical Daniela fashion, she went all in spending her time researching to understand climate change. As the magnitude of the problem became apparent, Daniela realized, "The world around me was not the world I thought it was." It seems apparent that we have a climate issue, but do we realize the severity of the problem? The oceans produce 50% of our oxygen, they are the primary resource of food for 3.5 billion people, and they control global weather patterns. But as quoted by the Sustainable Oceans Alliance, they are "threatened by marine pollution, ocean acidification, unsustainable fishing and habitat destruction."

The more time Daniela spent unpacking the problem, the more fear she felt, fear for the planet and fear for the next steps in her life. After graduating from Georgetown University, job offers were coming in, a dream in itself after growing up with little money and having low prospects of being accepted into a prestigious university. She was left conflicted with one of the most significant decisions to make in her life, a decision that seemed crystal clear based on her most trusted mentors' guidance: should she take the Wall Street job, work hard, and gain financial security (which she and her mom always sought)?

Fear was showing up in abundance, but a critical prompt paused her internal narrative: Am I doing this for myself or for others? Daniela knew in her heart that Wall Street was not right for her, but working on protecting and restoring our ocean was—and the Sustainable Oceans Alliance was born.

Where have I rocked it in life?

When working on massive global challenges, big promises and initiatives are required, at least from Daniela's perspective (who is well known for making bold promises in front of significant audiences). Her first promise was to hold an international summit of 150 young leaders alongside a meeting with the European Union in Malta. Her second big promise, again in front of a large audience, was to commit to launching the first-ever Ocean Solutions Accelerator program. In both situations, she did not have the capital to support the promise. In fact, she was nearing the end of any money she had left and did not know how she would do it.

What she did have was an unwavering sense of purpose, and she knew she could succeed: "I understood the power of knowing who I was, who I wanted to be, and knowing the thing I would do to get there." Daniela's sense of self and the awareness required to operate at this level is what I was most fascinated to unpack during our interview. When you can prime your mind in a way that is consistent with top-tier thinkers like Daniela, anything is possible.

Let's go back to the global stages where Daniela made bold promises. She felt the same level of fear any of us would, but relied on her heightened sense of self-awareness and belief in herself to rechannel panic and fear to fuel her promise and cause.

Daniela's process started with feeling that sense of fear, closing her eyes to see her vision, taking a deep breath, and reassuring herself that she and the people around her know precisely what needs to be done.

Reminding herself and triggering "self belief" is at the core of Daniela's visualization. It only takes seconds to unfold in the moment, but the mental training allowing for the visualization to execute flawlessly takes daily consistent effort. One of the best ways to foster self-belief is to constantly remind ourselves of what we have already accomplished in our lives.

I went through this exercise last night, as I'm about to start a new job with a significant portion of the role linked to sales performance. Fear crept up, and my best-selling internal narrative started to write a story centered around the fear of not hitting my objectives along with all the intricate details of how my life would unravel. Not cool. So I paused, took a few breaths, grabbed my notebook, and reminded myself of how I have excelled in jobs like this in the past. I reminded myself that there was no logical reason to be thinking through a lens of fear and that I had no evidence to support that story. The journaling only took minutes but saved me days of uncomfortable emotions, and better yet, left me feeling motivated and excited for this new job opportunity!

Think about where you have rocked it in life, and consciously write down those events and memories before a negative story writes itself without your permission. Keep this reflection close to you and revisit these words the next time you need a boost in self-confidence.

How can I prepare for the big moments in life?

When we exist in a fear state—scared, anxious, uncertain, or stuck—it's challenging to put in our best effort at life. I say life because it's not just our work performance being affected. Our ability to be that person we want to be is held back as if we are going through life pushing a boulder up a mountain. It's possible, but not pleasant. It will take longer to get to the top, and the chances of injury are much higher. In contrast, we can go up the same mountain by horseback, car, or land at the peak in a helicopter. There is no difference with our minds; tools are available.

Daniela's ability to shift and rechannel her fear, in what seems like seconds, is no accident. She trains her mind daily to do so. Her morning starts with movement and exercise. Think of physical activity in the morning as a kickstart to your system. If you're struggling with getting up early and feeling half asleep, do five pushups or air squats, and watch your body and mind come alive. It's a hack I use often, and I'm always amazed at the instant results.

Post exercise, Daniela meditates for fifteen to twenty minutes, then journals on the three main thoughts circulating in her mind. Combining meditation and journaling is a self-awareness super routine. Meditation slows your mind while journaling unpacks it. Meditation and journaling are by far the most common non-negotiable practices I have seen from interviews with top-level humans because they slow us down and bring us clarity.

When we notice our thoughts and understand our emotional triggers, we can bring the right tools to handle the situation. If faced with that steep mountain, I would much rather know that I have the ropes and carabiners to help me to the top. I might not need them, but I have them; and just knowing that gives me the confidence to take on the adventure.

One of the most potent non-negotiables in Daniela's life is training her mind to handle discomfort. She purposely puts herself in uncomfortable situations, like grand commitments to the UN on a stage in front of hundreds, making what is at first uncomfortable, now comfortable. This concept has come up with others when rechanneling fear. Ben Nemtin calls it "experience stacking" which I detail in his profile if you want to go deeper.

I feel one of those "easier said than done" comments coming from you right now. However, it is easier than you might think if you're training your mind daily like Daniela. Through her training, she is awarded confidence in knowing she can process and handle anything life throws her way while having the mental clarity to see the next steps forward.

I share Daniela's mental fitness routine to show there is nothing new or unattainable in her flow. At this point in the book, we have covered in detail every practice Daniela uses. Now it's up to you to experiment and understand what types of training will prepare you best for those big life moments, ones that spark fear and have the potential to cripple our progress if let unattended.

What mental fitness will you implement tomorrow morning, or even better, right now?

Final Thought

Don't retreat. Instead, rechannel.

How can I think different?

Steve Jobs

Reinvented how we think about products, design, and technology

February 24, 1955 – October 5, 2011

QUICK BIO

- Entrepreneur who cofounded Apple with Steve Wozniak in 1976
- Left Apple (1985) and acquired a controlling interest in Pixar (1986), a computer graphics company that was part of Lucasfilm Ltd. Pixar was later sold to The Walt Disney Company (2006)
- Steve went back to Apple (1996) as a consultant and started leading the company once again the following year
- He was instrumental in engineering the award-winning advertising campaign "Think Different"
- Reinvented Apple (and complete industries) in the 21st century by introducing iTunes (music software), the iPod (portable MP3 player), and the iPhone (mobile telephone)
- Due to health concerns, he resigned as CEO (2011) becoming chairman, then passed away two months later
- Had an interest in Buddhism early on in his life after going on a pilgrimage to India to experience Buddhism

Behind the Question

Steve Jobs was different. He was a person that many loved and some hated, but all could appreciate and respect one thing—his mind. Steve thought differently, saw what others could not see, and reimagined what was possible. Using technology, he transformed entire industries and how we live, creating things that not long ago were pure fantasy. Perhaps the most valuable transformation Steve left us with was changing the way we think. Here is the copy (that Steve also helped write) from Apple's original 1997 "Think Different" advertising campaign:

> *"Here's to the crazy ones, the misfits, the rebels, the troublemakers, the round pegs in the square holes...the ones who see things differently—they're not fond of rules... You can quote them, disagree with them, glorify or vilify them, but the only thing you can't do is ignore them because they change things... They push the human race forward, and while some may see them as the crazy ones, we see genius, because the ones who are crazy enough to think that they can change the world, are the ones who do." — Steve Jobs, 1997*

I, for one, am thankful. The words you are reading are a result of Steve thinking differently and pushing the entire team at Apple to do the same. I type these words on my MacBook while listening to music through my AirPods, and will later outline another profile using my iPad and Apple pencil. The best part is everything works seamlessly together allowing me to work efficiently and from any place in the world.

Steve made an important distinction, "Everything around

you that you call life was made up by people that were no smarter than you." We all have the potential to create change and to inspire others along the way. So, how can we think differently just like Steve Jobs? As it turns out, it's all about the questions we ask. To think differently, we have to ask different questions. To ask different questions, we require "the pause."

Where can I pause to think?

The pause is where the magic lives. Most people travel right through it on autopilot, but in that pause is where things change and go from average to extraordinary. As the author of Steve Jobs's biography, Walter Isaacson explained, "During the development of almost every product he ever created, Jobs at a certain point hit the pause button and went back to the drawing board because he felt it wasn't perfect." Most people would continue and follow the plan even when their intuition was telling them something different. Steve himself would pause, but he also showed his team what was possible when they stopped to think.

Larry Kenyon, an engineer, working on the Macintosh operating system, was challenged to speed up the system. Steve reframed the challenge and asked, "If it would save a person's life, could you find a way to shave 10 seconds off the boot time?" He went on to do the math and show Larry he could save 300 million hours a year for 5 million people by saving them ten seconds each day. From one pause, and one question, Larry came back with a machine booting up twenty-eight seconds faster.

We all have areas in our professional and personal lives where we could use a pause to think, to question, and to come out better on the other side. Now is the time to take that pause.

Where in your life could you slow down to think? Reflect on the projects, activities, and life decisions that would benefit from thinking like Steve Jobs. With these areas of your life identified, I would suggest firing up deeper thinking early in the morning when your mind is most fresh, free of distraction, and has not been influenced by events of the day. We can also leverage what we know about Steve and his way of thinking to help solve our own challenges. What would Steve do in your situation?

Think of where Steve would pause to think and the questions he might ask. I am willing to bet you will be surprised by what surfaces. Sometimes it just takes a slight shift in perspective to unlock a completely different view. Maya Angelou also used this technique to think through challenging situations. Maya would reflect on what her grandmother would do if she were in the same situation. You, I, and everyone else have the same opportunity to think differently, just like the great Steve Jobs. Go for it!

How do I get others to think differently?

Steve once said, "I hate the way people use slide presentations instead of thinking." Using slides, Steve has delivered some of the most stunning and impactful presentations and product launches of our time. But he used them as a visual companion versus emptying everything in his mind hoping that others could make sense of it. Anyone who has worked in the corporate world has likely sat through a fifty-slide (or more) presentation looking like a mental grenade exploded in the deck. Steve did everything possible to get everyone around him to think differently. When this happens, better products and experiences are created.

"Creativity comes from spontaneous meetings from random discussions. You run into someone, and you ask what they're doing, you say 'wow,' and soon you're cooking up all sorts of ideas." Steve had the Pixar building designed to funnel people through the central atrium, resulting in spontaneous meetings that sparked all sorts of new ideas. The more you exercise your mental muscles to think differently (by pausing and asking questions) and doing so in front of others, the more likely they will start doing the same. I believe this is a huge reason people showed unwavering loyalty to Steve Jobs even when he was not the most comfortable human to be working around. As Debi Coleman (previous Chief Financial Officer at Apple) recalls, "He would shout at a meeting, 'You asshole, you never do anything right,' yet I consider myself the absolute luckiest person in the world to have worked with him."

When you are creating and thinking at your best while surrounded by others doing the same, you also feel awesome. There is a palpable energy that keeps looping, giving rise to excitement, motivation, and inspiration. Thinking differently is a skill and mental superpower that follows us forever. It pushes our minds to operate at elite levels while inspiring others to do the same. Everyone wins. Steve Jobs may no longer physically be with us, but the result of him thinking differently is experienced by us daily through the products and services he helped bring to our world.

How do I know when to pause?

Intuitively, we know when to pause if we consistently train our minds with any of the practices mentioned within this book. It has worked for the humans behind these profiles and can work for you. As publicly known as Steve is, many remain unaware of a critical element that he mastered, one which allowed him to pause and think differently. As detailed in an *Inc.* magazine story, "Steve Jobs was a pioneer in what was once a rather esoteric 'mind technology'—the use of Zen mindfulness meditation to reduce his stress, gain more clarity, and enhance his creativity."

Fortunately, having a mindfulness practice is no longer a vague idea as mainstream society has heard enough of the benefits. However, from what I see through my interviews and working individually with people, finding a personalized mental fitness routine and consistently practicing that routine is still a problem.

I hope to share many angles and practices through these profiles, because all it takes is one core practice or one question to land and kickstart your mental fitness. The techniques that work for me, Steve Jobs, or anyone else featured in the book work because they resonate with us individually. Keep exploring and challenging your mind with progressive questions, and be ready for extraordinary benefits and unexpected opportunities to show up.

Why not start now with trying out Steve's mindfulness practice? His mindfulness meditation focused on the breath and observing his thoughts, looking something like this: sit cross-legged, with your eyes closed, focus on your breath. The monkey mind of racing thoughts will fire up, but over time, and being present with your breath, those thoughts will start to calm down. If you are brand new to meditation, I have found apps like Calm, Headspace, or Ten Percent Happier to be great starting points. They have expert teachers (including Jeff Warren) to help get you started. Personally, I like to extend the practice on my own in silence for a combined total of fifteen or twenty minutes.

When you find the style of meditation that works for you, as reported by Steve, "Your mind just slows down, and you see a tremendous expanse in the moment. You see so much more than you could see before." Part of seeing more than you could before is in the pause and knowing when to take it.

At this point in the book, you have everything you need to do this! Leverage and personalize Steve's world-class mental fitness formula to boost your self-awareness. The moments to pause are all there, you just need to see and take them.

Final Thought

Think different by knowing when to pause.

How can I think different?

Where can I release self-doubt?

Sarah Davidson

Lawyer turned multi-million dollar entrepreneur

QUICK BIO

- Entrepreneur and Founder of Matcha Maiden green tea, a multimillion-dollar company operating globally
- Started her first business after suffering from a case of complete adrenal exhaustion
- Author and host of the popular podcast *Seize the Yay*, investigating how some of the world's most inspiring people find their "yay"

"I wouldn't say I'm the best candidate for a 'short bio' because I'm not only a serial rambler but also an over-enthusiastic life-lover with too many interests, passions, career changes, personal transformations, lifestyle revelations, adventures, hopes and dreams for one single lifetime. I nonetheless do my very best to squeeze in as much goal-kicking, ground-breaking and memory-making as life permits and I'd say I'm best summed up by my overarching life philosophy—'seize the yay.'" —Sarah Davidson

Behind the Question

Sarah often describes herself as a "funtrapreneur," which at first made me think, "Who can describe herself as a funtrapreneur and still build a multimillion-dollar business?" Sarah can, that's who! It did not take long for me to drop my judgments of whom I thought an entrepreneur should be and realized that Sarah, a brilliant, kind, fun human who immediately brings a smile to my face, has created her own category to operate in business.

"So many of us live without questioning whether we could live better, but life is too short not to enjoy to the fullest." This is Sarah in a nutshell. Someone who shows up with passion, confidence, and a zest for life that leaves people walking away energized and ready to take on the world. But, guess what? Sarah is human like the rest of us and has worked through self-doubt to leave her job as a lawyer and go all in as an entrepreneur. In conversation about her matcha tea company idea, Sarah would preface by saying, "I've got this really crap idea that's probably not going to work...." Those are some pretty strong words pointed in the opposite direction of where her life and business ended up heading.

So what changed? On the other side of the negativity was the person described in this profile. She had to short circuit the natural human condition of self-doubt to access the hugely successful funtrapreneur many know today. Sarah starts by acknowledging that self-doubt is normal and a part of being human. I've seen this approach from others when working through anxiety and fear. For example, Jeff Warren, meditation teacher and co-author with *ABC News* anchor Dan Harris of *Meditation For Fidgety Skeptics*, often says, "Welcome to the party," when acknowledging unwanted feelings and emotions as they arrive. It's a part of being human and living.

Sarah accepts self-doubt as a natural human instinct, but has learned to allow for more space between her thoughts and decisions. Treat self-doubt as another one of those narratives running through our minds that is often false and unjustified. When we can disconnect or zoom out to 30,000 feet outside of the noise, we have the best shot at making decisions and taking actions that are not influenced by the narrative. Do not be alarmed when self-doubt shows up again. This is normal, but the more we train our minds, the faster we can move over to the other side, where opportunity lives.

Try this: List the self-doubts showing up right now in your life. With the narrative paused, acknowledge these thoughts on the page. Reflect on how your limiting beliefs are affecting the decisions and actions you are taking. Now you can see everything together on one page and how your amazing potential is being held back from the world because of the narratives in front of your eyes. Once you complete the exercise, you can write "Thank you for coming to the party, but you'll have to leave now," or whatever feels right to release these thoughts and focus on the next steps.

As Sarah says, "Everything you do is a mental exercise. The first thing is getting over the mental hurdle." When you do this once, you'll do it again with more ease, continually raising the bar of possibility. Go for it!

"Doubt kills more dreams than failure ever will."
—*Sarah Davidson*

Is my passion burning me out?

Okay, so we remove self-doubt from holding us back and doing the things we have always wanted to do, but there can be an expected byproduct to this situation. A newfound release of passion often shows up, that if not managed can also be destructive. I like to think of this as "passion burnout" which Sarah experienced after leaving her corporate job to start Matcha Maiden.

As you train your mind in self-awareness, you will be able to see and feel this type of burnout creeping up, and you can correct your course—something I lived firsthand (more on that later). I think anyone can relate to the stresses and demands that corporate life can produce. Not all companies, let's be fair, but many still work their employees with crazy timelines, deliverables, and often ignoring working-hour boundaries to the point of burnout.

The same situation can develop if you leave the corporate world to start your entrepreneurial journey. It can actually be worse. In Sarah's case, she worked through self-doubt and found her passion. She rarely wanted to stop building her new business and could not justify taking a break. Why? "Because it doesn't feel like work," says Sarah. This is just one example, but there are many others—such as putting everything on the line and feeling that you have to work 24/7 to make the business succeed, or have the pressure of paying your team's salaries knowing their livelihood is counting on your business's success.

No matter the situation, they all lead to the same thing—pushing your mind and body to a breaking point. This is the scenario we hear of most, but before the explosion of tension erupts, something else happens that makes everything worse.

We jam our minds with decisions and expectations as if we were filling up a storage room floor to ceiling with boxes. In my opinion, this is the critical turning point where one decision can avoid the burnout or fuel it. Clear out your mind.

Sarah says it best, "If there is no space, there is no opportunity." You can't see the opportunity, and even if you can, you no longer have the mental capacity to take advantage of that opportunity. It's not complicated. We can't perform at our best when we can't see the steps in front of us, and the longer that goes on, the more our storage locker fills up. At some point, when we unlock the door, everything comes crashing down on us—and we are forced to clean up the mess.

We can avoid that mess in the first place by scheduling self-maintenance time, something that Sarah has made a non-negotiable in her life. For Sarah, meditating twice a day, exercising, taking gentle walks, implementing no-phone Sundays, getting out of the city once a month, and not working after dinner are just some of the self-maintenance strategies she has implemented.

Sarah left me with a prompt that we can all use to identify our self-maintenance strategies: What are all the ways you can bring better work hygiene to your life?

Let's think about this. List everything that will make your work hygiene world class. To be clear, this is not only for entrepreneurs. While you are going through this exercise, you can draw on the "happiness list exercise" presented in Nikki Sharp's profile. Both practices will inspire and complement each other.

"You've got to get the mind right first before anything else follows," says Sarah. When you do, get ready for a thriving personal and professional life!

Final Thought

Unthinkable success and opportunity live behind self-doubt.

Has this happened before?

Jason Feifer
Editor in Chief of *Entrepreneur* Magazine

QUICK BIO

- Editor in Chief of *Entrepreneur* magazine, previously an editor at *Men's Health*, *Fast Company*, *Maxim*, and *Boston* magazine
- Host of three podcasts: *Build For Tomorrow*, a history show about why people resist new things; *Hush Money*, about all the ways money makes life awkward; and *Problem Solvers*, about how entrepreneurs solve unexpected problems in their business
- Wrote a novel with his wife (*Mr. Nice Guy*) which is being developed for television

---

Behind the Question

Editor of a huge magazine, author of a novel, author of a non-fiction book in the works, host of three podcasts, father, and a husband. Holy shit! That was my first thought before hitting "record" for my interview with Jason. I immediately got the impression he was incredibly efficient with his time, so I was not interested in how he physically managed everything, but how he mentally handled it.

From our conversation, and the themes coming out of Jason's work, three main factors surfaced as the answer to my question:

1. Get grounded.
2. Get clear.
3. Get intentional.

The themes I picked up on from Jason and the structure of this book are nearly a perfect mirror. The only thing that appears to be missing is the "expansion of possibility," but it's actually not missing at all. If you are grounded, clear, and intentional, possibility and expansion follow. It's why Jason's profile is in part three of the book!

Jason's podcast, *Build For Tomorrow* (formerly *Pessimists Archive*), is a perfect example and tool to help get grounded. The show unpacks the stories of how people resisted change across history. Through these examples, we clearly and quickly realize that everything we are struggling with right now has happened before.

I am going on the record to warn you that there is some serious potential of getting sucked into the infinite scroll if you jump into the show's Instagram account (@pessimistsarc). Explore a feed full of examples of what appears ridiculous today, but were serious conversations then. Be ready for your eyes to open wide and for uncontrolled blurting of things like, "No way! You're kidding! Yeah, right!" I get it. I was there too, but don't say I didn't warn you:

Radio Blamed For Insomnia (1926)
*Doctors are complaining, college presidents are
lamenting, mothers are tearing their hair! It's radio, again.*

Bicycle Blamed for Appendicitis (Chicago Tribune, 1905)
"Washington physician claims disease is the result of riding."

2020: *"Too much phone"*
1985: *"Too much gaming"*
1950: *"Too many comics"*
1863: *"Too much reading"*

William F. Buckley Jr. on home PC (1982)
"Do We Really Need Home Computers?

Really? But at the time, I am sure, these headlines and newspaper articles (from reputable newspapers) were striking up a lot of thought and discussion and did not seem as far-fetched as they appear today.

The reality being, what bothers us now bothered someone else before, or to Jason's point, "We repeat ourselves over time." This is where the grounding comes in. We can take comfort in knowing we are not alone in the way we are feeling and can apply this thinking to process challenging situations. People have figured out many challenges in the past, and we have those same capabilities.

*"You can move forward knowing that not all
things will fall apart." —Jason Feifer*

Here's the thing with this mental hack: it slows the internal narrative, calms the fear, and allows us to pause and use that powerful thing sitting on top of our shoulders—our mind. When we pause, we clear out the mental fog, think more clearly, and allow for solutions to surface. As Naveen Jain often says, "Anything is possible."

Try this: Think about the challenges in your life or the things you fear most right now. Get specific, pick one, and write down all the details about the situation. Then step back, take a walk, let these thoughts sit. Come back to them with a fresh mind and ask: Has this happened before? Think about situations from the past that resemble what you described. What happened in those examples? What was causing the fear? What was the solution?

Often, just going through this process will calm our fear and anxiety allowing solutions to surface. The byproduct of understanding solutions from other challenges is a perspective shift, the ability to see and approach your challenge through another lens. History repeats itself. Why not learn from the bright minds of our past? Be open, explore, and enjoy it!

What am I missing?

Looking back in time and using history to help shift our perspective can naturally lead to a powerful follow-up prompt: What am I missing? Jason often leverages this question when mentally jammed on a challenge. He ran up against a mental block while trying to structure and title his latest nonfiction book:

"Can I just take every single thought I've ever had and put those aside and look at it in a completely different way?"

Sometimes we just need to reset our mind. Think of this reset in the same light as restarting your phone or computer after days, weeks, or months of operating. Too many programs and tasks are running at the same time. Hit restart and take on the challenge with a fresh mind.

Now, how do we do this? I would pair up the prompts Jason uses (*What am I missing? And where is the more significant opportunity?*) with another mental clearing activity, an activity or practice that you know will help clear your mind and leave you feeling refreshed. My go-to's are long walks and Peloton spin classes. (Let's just say I've been doing a lot of walking and spinning while writing this book!) Do your mind clearing activity first, then sit down with the prompts and unpack your challenge to get past the surface and find that thing, thought, or idea that will make the real difference.

> *"The thing that I have is not the thing that I need. The thing that I have is just the starter point. But the thing that is really going to make a difference is not in front of me or in my head yet, so I need to be searching for that." —Jason Feifer*

Finding that "thing" is what will take us from good to great and from average to world class. The unlock is available to us all when using practices to create space in our minds and prompts to push our thinking to unexplored realms.

What should result from this moment?

The last Jason Feifer superpower is showing up with intentional focus and being critical and deliberate with your time. When we do this, we can host multiple podcasts, write books, and be the editor in chief of Entrepreneur magazine! We can accomplish an abundance when we are grounded, clear, and intentional.

"What should result from this moment?" is a solid prompt to help dial in our intentionality. Think about a week, a month, or a year from now. The time you are currently spending on a task directly affects what you will have and how you will feel in the future. The time you are spending right now reading these pages, I hope, will yield nothing but pure awesomeness and future opportunity from incorporating reflective practices into your routine.

Make sure to be conscious of what you want in the future when planning out your days and weeks. If the activities in your calendar do not support what you want in your life, something has to change. Our priorities, desires, and ambitions shift over time, but so should our habits to support them. Often we get stuck in outdated patterns simply because we have been in the pattern for an extended period, and it feels comfortable.

I regularly audit my calendar to help ensure I'm not getting stuck in these patterns. It's easy to slip into autopilot. It's happening to me right now. Today, as I write this profile in the early morning, I know I have a day packed to the brim with thirty-minute introduction/business development calls. I'm sure they will lead to great conversations with stunning humans, but they do not support my top priorities for the next few months. So, I've adjusted my calendar for next week to better balance these meetings while ensuring I have the time I need to focus on my top priorities.

That's it, I'm not beating myself up over the situation, but I am also ensuring that the pattern does not continue. Thank you, Jason, because your prompts paused my autopilot and allowed me to be more grounded, clear, and intentional. I hope they do the same for all of you.

Final Thought

The world may look and feel different today, but in reality, it's not that different at all.

Has this happened before?

Who's showing up to my party?

Jeff Warren
The no-bullshit meditation guy

QUICK BIO

- Coauthor, along with Dan Harris and Carlye Adler, of *Meditation for Fidgety Skeptics*
- Author of *The Head Trip* published by Random House in 2007, and was recently named among the top ten books about consciousness by *The Guardian*
- Can find his guided meditations on the Ten Percent Happier and Calm apps
- Founder of The Consciousness Explorers Club (CEC), a meditation think tank and community hub
- Mission is to empower people to take charge of their own mental health through the creative application of meditation and personal growth practices

"I make meditation and practice accessible to diverse audiences in order to help people live more sane lives. I've taught meditation to US Army cadets, the Royal Canadian Mounted Police, Arizona cops, Google executives, distractible teens, suspicious journalists, burned-out caregivers,

formerly-incarcerated youth, and every other conceivable demographic of freethinkers, including squirmy six-year-old kids. I try to do this in a way that's rigorous and clear and adventurous. You can sit with me every week via my live "'Do Nothing Project' on YouTube." —Jeff Warren

Behind the Question

I interviewed Jeff Warren once, yet he sits on my shoulder daily as a subconscious voice and reminder that it's okay to have unwanted guests at my party. My conversation with Jeff started with him sharing that he defines himself by the relationships in his life. "Our communities reflect back at us," he shared. The conversation came full circle when I asked my final question: "Jeff, what truly makes you smile each day?" He replied, "I like people. They make me smile."

People and relationships are essential to Jeff, and, I would argue, the relationships with the "unwanted people" in his life are some of the most important. I know they have been for me. Let me explain. Jeff is a globally recognized teacher making meditation and mindfulness more accessible through his unique narrative and humorous style. Just read a few lines out of his book *Meditation For Fidgety Skeptics*, and you'll see what I mean!

His lighthearted approach to identifying thoughts, and the emotions charging those thoughts, immediately softens a situation. He has the ability to shift experiences commonly causing stress and anxiety to more welcoming and accepting emotions, ultimately making us feel a hell of a lot better!

As Jeff would say when it comes to emotions, "Welcome to the party." Naming emotions is a great way to pause the looping narrative that typically fires up in these situations. This is where the "Jeff on my shoulder" comes into play. Whenever unwanted emotions show up in my mind, I can hear Jeff saying something like, "Oh, look who just arrived! It's Fearful John and Anxious Linda!" No disrespect to any Johns or Lindas reading these words!

The name is less important than the labelling of the emotion to disconnect it from running the show. You are not Anxious Linda, she just happens to be in the room with you, which is okay. "You're accepting the world is having an impact on you," Jeff reminds us. To change or to minimize the effects of these unwanted party guests, we first have to accept that they are at the party in the first place—not push them to the corner of the room, hoping they will leave on their own.

Start with tuning into your body. When unwanted emotions arise, reflect on where they are showing up. Take out that pen and paper again and write out the details. Think about the story or delusion you might be in during these moments. Don't forget to put a name to the emotions!

Journaling alone will help pause the narrative and diffuse the emotional reactions. Meditation serves as an in-the-moment calming tool and increases your self-awareness. This makes it easier to spot and accept emotions as they come to you. I would highly recommend reading Jeff's books, trying one of his workshops, or taking any of his guided meditations in both the Calm and Ten Percent Happier apps.

Can I find comfort in my discomfort?

Accepting your house party guests and the temporary discomfort they bring trains your mind to tolerate discomfort and see the contrast in the highs and lows of life. These practices go both ways, addressing the negatives but also opening up the positives.

Having the mental clarity and capacity to manage your houseguests, or thoughts and emotions, also frees up space to see what has always been there. Now that we have ushered out the mental noise, we can be more present with the details in front of us.

"As you begin to get more clear, as you begin to start to pay attention to these subtitles, then the world expands—your consciousness expands." —Jeff Warren

Personally speaking, being committed to mental fitness practices has genuinely expanded my world—what I see, feel, and experience—like going through life with 3D vision. Making decisions has become easier, more obvious, and leaves me feeling aligned. For example, when I first spoke to the CEO of Baronfig about the idea for this book and an offer was made to publish, the answer was a hell yes! All the signs pointed to that response because my mind was clear enough to see them in the first place.

It's the small details that accumulate and produce tremendous results. Jeff shared a simple example of just noticing the sun lighting up the leaves and taking a moment to let that pleasure sink in. Every moment can have that freshness to it, and it makes for beautiful days.

Think of the moments in your day-to-day life that you may be rushing through. Or, catch yourself the next time you notice something interesting. Pause and, as Jeff left with me, "Let it land, let it land, let it land." Take it all in! You may not notice it right away, but as you continue to take in the details, like the water running down your arms in the shower, you will start seeing more detail—and the *right* details—in your work and life, allowing you to make better decisions to live life to the fullest.

Final Thought

All are welcome to my party, but some guests can stay longer than others.

Who's showing up to my party?

Who am I without this thought?

Jill Wintersteen

Works at the intersection of neuroscience and astrology

QUICK BIO

- Founder of Spirit Daughter, a 1.2 million-person community designed to help people live their best lives
- Astrology and yoga have served as the foundation of her life for over twenty years
- While studying neuroscience at John Hopkins, a move to Venice Beach to study Chinese medicine presented itself and revealed her true calling: helping others find grounding, peace, and their path

---

Behind the Question

I reached out to Jill in 2018 for an interview because she's an awesome human, first and foremost, and secondly, to learn from her wisdom in astrology to help open people up to new and different ways of thinking. Her knowledge would help me better understand the practices and energies we could leverage to live our best lives.

I say new, but when talking about astrology, it could not be anything further from new, dating back over 25,000 years when some of the first lunar cycles were noted on cave walls. Before I met Jill, I knew very little about astrology, and by default was a skeptic to energy work. In retrospect, it was a disservice to myself. I don't know where you stand on this topic, but all I ask is you take in and reflect on this profile with an open mind.

We have many daily thoughts. Some thoughts are great, others are debilitating. By default we are still wired to survive, which leads to more fight-or-flight-based thoughts than happy ones. The good news is we can shift this pattern of thinking through sharp prompts and leveraged moon cycles. Before we can get there, we need to recognize that we are more than our thoughts, hence the opening prompt. All thoughts are temporary; and from this perspective, we can spend time understanding who we are without the mix of thoughts that confuse and scramble the mind.

Try this: Grab two pieces of paper. Write down all the thoughts and emotions coming up for you right now on one of the pages. These can be thoughts causing you stress or happiness. It's not a good or bad exercise, it's an *everything*-related-to-thoughts exercise. Set that paper aside. On the other page, reflect on the characteristics that make you proud of yourself and define you as the human you are. Before you put pen to paper, smile. I mean it, physically smile and feel the effects of that smile. See yourself in a beautiful light with an untouchable aura. Now, write down your incredible characteristics.

You have two pieces of paper in front of you. One with the characteristics that make up the exceptional human you are, the other with thoughts, feelings, and emotions that will always come and go. Take the thought page—rip it up, set it on fire, recycle it, whatever feels right for you, but physically and mentally release it. Now you are left with one page of characteristics reflecting the stunning human you are. Keep this page as a reference to shift your mood when needed.

We often think of these exercises only to release thoughts causing pain, but it's important to include all thoughts and emotions. Regardless of exactly what's brewing in the mind, it's the association, or the dependence on that thought that we are releasing. Let me illustrate the point using an example from the Netflix documentary *The Last Dance*, profiling the life of Michael Jordan.

After six years of back-to-back NBA championships, head coach Phil Jackson called the final team meeting. The year would be known as the last dance, the last time some of the best players in the league like Michael Jordan, Scottie Pippen, Steve Kerr, and Dennis Rodman would ever play together. Phil asked each player to come to that meeting with a piece of paper filled with the words and thoughts signifying what the team meant to them. Those papers were then dropped into a tin can and lit on fire. This was an experience to reflect on the memories created together. It was an opportunity to bring closure while allowing everyone to move forward to their next phase of life. Steve Kerr described the burning of the notes as "one of the most powerful things I've ever seen."

Use this moment right now to release, bring closure, or step into a new phase of living—whatever you need right now to clear your head. Think of your mind as a physical room where you open the doors in order to clear the space and freshen the air. Now that we've cleaned out our minds, we can start to get clear and intentional with our journey. In Jill's words, "I believe that once we get really clear, start calling in the right energy, and align with our intentions that things just speed up."

How can I limit uncertainty?

In my conversation with Jill, she spoke a lot about the fear of the unknown, something I know we can all appreciate. Our lives are filled with the unknown: understanding where we will be five years from now, how that product will do when launched, who will be in our lives, where we might be living, or frankly, what may show up today. We can make assumptions or predictions on what may happen, but we really don't know, which can be scary.

Jill has a rock solid and simple strategy to navigate the uncertainty we all face. She gets crystal clear in her mind. "You can become so clear that you are willing to get uncomfortable." The daily practice Jill uses to bring this clarity to her life is quite simple, but can change everything and propel us to realizing our dreams. She lists five things she wants to do today and five things she eventually wants to do. I know you may be thinking, "Wait a minute, surely this can't be it." Yes it is, because it's easier to stay on track when the practice or habit is simple to execute.

It's the starting point in seeing the themes that continue to surface during your daily reflection. Maybe things like writing a book, starting a podcast, or competing in a triathlon keep showing up on your "five things you eventually want to do" list. Whatever it is for you, seeing it day in and day out will give you the confidence required to take the first steps in realizing those dreams. Jill believes, "Once we are really clear in what our dreams are, that's what propels us to take a leap."

Uncertainty and the unknown will still be present throughout the journey between now and accomplishing the items on your list, but knowing where you're heading will help you navigate through that uncertainty. You start to become "comfortable with being uncomfortable, because you know there is a purpose to it," says Jill.

This may all seem overly simplistic, and that's the point. We have this strange societal relationship with complexity, assuming that complexity dictates the size of the impact that the project will have. There is some truth to this, but even the largest projects, like the ones that can impact a billion people (see Naveen Jain's profile) are executed through microsteps leading toward the end goal.

Our life, the biggest project of them all, is no different. It starts with releasing the thoughts holding us back so we can then get clear on where we want to be heading. Now, we execute toward our desires while leveraging the tools and practices scattered throughout all of these profiles to help get us there.

How can I leverage the natural energy of the moon?

First, I need to be completely transparent regarding what I talk about when it comes to the moon and the energy flowing through us. I'm not an expert and have only a fraction of the knowledge that Jill possesses. My goal is not to write a mini astrology profile but instead to pique your curiosity and stimulate you to learn more about what is possible.

Through her work and wisdom, Jill is the one who can feed our curiosity. Her understanding and expertise in astrology and neuroscience is a perfect combination to teach us and the 1.2

million people following her work at Spirit Daughter.

My perspective and understanding of the relationship between cosmic energy and our mental fitness are simple. There is only an upside to being led by the astrological themes of the months and cycles. Let's look at an example I pulled straight from Spirit Daughter's Instagram account:

"The Moon lands in Gemini today, quickening our mind and energy. It's important to focus on what's most important or distractions will pop up from every angle. See your day unfolding then attempt to say no to anything that doesn't fit your vision. Send energy where you want to and don't allow anything to take it from you without your permission. You can accomplish great things with the Moon in Gemini, as long as you focus your energy." —@spiritdaughter, October 7, 2020

We can all win by eliminating distractions and increasing our focus. Even if you have zero understanding of astrology, allowing yourself to be guided by the energetic themes that the discipline provides will further deepen our practices.

Suppose you are starting to implement the practices outlined in this book, such as slowing down to think, taking time to be intentional, or working on releasing mental blocks and limiting beliefs. Why not level up the whole experience by aligning with the natural energy surrounding us? We are already experimenting, so I see no downside to finding more focus with our questions, intentions, and affirmations based on energetic themes unfolding.

Jill has a beautiful perspective, "The energy presented to

us through the cosmos are just opportunities, and we have the choice to tap into them or not." I'll leave you with one other example from Jill's work through her *Moon Journals* (which I highly recommend):

> *"The New Moon is the beginning of a new Lunar Cycle. It is a time of fresh starts, inward contemplation, and realignment with our path. Each month, the Moon meets the Sun in the sky, and they join forces to create a spark of energy that we can harness. Under the New Moon, we are cosmically supported in setting intentions and creating affirmations that we can carry through the entire Lunar Cycle, creating a blueprint for our life.*
>
> *If we choose to follow this blueprint each month, we slowly change our life one New Moon at a time. Not everything may change at once, but if we stay committed to our intentions set on the New Moon, our life begins to take on our design. Our visions come to life and the shifts we make, create lasting patterns, providing a foundation for the next step on our journey."* —New Moon, April 22, 2020

We have come full circle with this profile, thanks to Jill's inspiration and knowledge, by first understanding that we are more significant than the thoughts coming and going in our mind. Second, by getting crystal clear with our dreams and intentions we can shut down fear and welcome the uncomfortable. And finally, we pull all our practices and reflection together with the support of the cosmos.

Final Thought

The energy of the cosmos and our thoughts coexist harmoniously.

What world do I want to create?

J.R.R. Tolkien

Globally-bestselling author of the Lord of the Rings series

January 3, 1892 – September 2, 1973

QUICK BIO

- John Ronald Reuel Tolkien was an English fantasy writer, poet, philologist, and academic
- Published globally-renowned novels such as *The Hobbit* and *The Lord of the Rings* trilogy while teaching at Oxford University
- Studied English language at Exeter College in Oxford, inventing his own languages for his novels
- Was a lieutenant in the First World War which inspired his later writing
- Was made a Commander of the Order of the British Empire in the 1972 New Year Honours, and in the same year received the insignia of the Order at Buckingham Palace, while Oxford University also gave him an honorary Doctorate of Letters

---

Behind the Question

J. R. R. Tolkien was an Oxford University English language and literature professor. On the side, he was an author of books that have sold over 150 million copies. That's a serious side hustle!

Let's set the stage. Below is the opening to one of Tolkien's "walking songs," which are used in a variety of ways throughout his books.

> *"Still round the corner there may wait*
> *A new road or a secret gate,*
> *And though I oft have passed them by,*
> *A day will come at last when I*
> *Shall take the hidden paths that run*
> *West of the Moon, East of the Sun."*
> —J. R. R. Tolkien

What I love about Tolkien's work is exactly what fuels this profile: opening up our minds and lives to new perspectives and possibilities through experiencing different worlds. Real or fictitious doesn't matter. These worlds, paths, experiences, and reflections allow us to leave our default world behind and explore new possibilities. When we stimulate our imagination, opportunity is typically close behind.

Let's go on a creative reflective exercise that may seem like an irrational experience, but has a great chance of revealing rational observations. Time to create your J. R. R. Tolkien world. You do not have to write a fantasy book (although nothing stops you from doing so), but instead allow yourself to draw or bullet point the story you would love to live out. Think about yourself as the main character of your story, the world your story takes place in, and the characters involved. No rules, no judgement, just free thinking.

"Fairy tales do not deny the existence of sorrow and failure: the possibility of these is necessary to the joy of deliverance. It denies (in the face of much evidence, if you will) universal final defeat...giving a fleeting glimpse of Joy; Joy beyond the walls of the world, poignant as grief." —*J. R. R. Tolkien*

I share the quote above because I'm not proposing we escape our current realities, but more so take a break from them. Let our minds flow free, without stress, while stimulating creative thought. Living in a society obsessed with productivity, we rarely allow ourselves to explore creative thinking without a goal associated with the process. Here's your chance. Go for it! Remember to keep the process simple so that it is inviting enough that you actually do it. My story consisted of bullet points covering one 8.5 by 11-inch sheet of paper. That's it. And for some, I am sure, you will write more; but for me, that's all I needed to get started and draw insight into what my story was trying to tell me.

This one line, "In a hole in the ground there lived a hobbit," written down by J. R. R. Tolkien while grading English papers, was the line that started what is now an empire of fantasy stories that have been consumed by millions around the world and across generations. I cannot say our stories will yield the same results, but I know we can learn from the words put down on paper.

What is your story telling you?

My story revolved around time travel, back in history and forward into the future. I was experiencing different worlds, cultures, life forms, and moments in time within the blink of an eye. I would come back to my world and share the wisdom gathered with the village I lived in. I say village because the experience I imagined involved a small group of people living deep in the forest, but with cutting-edge technology and modern amenities.

I'll stop sharing the details of my fictional story before I lose you. I know, I should stick to nonfiction—but the point is that in only minutes of letting my mind run wild on one sheet of paper, I came away with this:

- I enjoy travel and experiences abroad.
- Sharing what I learn is important to me.
- Delivering teachings uniquely and creatively energizes and motivates me.

The results of an exercise like this can vary, from exercising your creative muscles to bringing awareness, as it did for me, to areas in your life where you can expand, develop, and come up with new ideas. Think about the story you mapped out and what it may be telling you. Maybe merely going through the process felt freeing, refreshing, and gave you a well-deserved mental break. That's equally valuable!

As J. R. R. Tolkien famously said, "Not all those who wander are lost." Let's all take some time to wander and see where it takes us.

Final Thought

There are the worlds we live in now and the worlds we can live in later.

How can I mentally outwork my opponents?

Apolo Ohno

United States of America's most decorated winter Olympian

QUICK BIO

- Claimed first major speed skating title at the US Championships at the age of fourteen after only six months of training
- Earned eight Olympic medals in short track speed skating across the 2002, 2006, and 2010 Winter Games
- *New York Times* best-selling author and global speaker
- Completed the 2014 Ironman World Championship Triathlon in Kona, Hawaii, in less than ten hours

------

Behind the Question

Apolo Ohno is an eight-time Olympic medalist in short track speed skating. After my interview with him, something else became very clear to me: he is and will forever be a gold medalist in mental fitness.

> *"The visualization process was so rich in detail and layer I could begin sweating while I was meditating on a flight."*
> —*Apolo Ohno*

Can you imagine sitting next to Apolo on a flight, eyes closed and beads of sweat starting to form on his face? The first thing that would come to my mind is that this guy is going to vomit at any point—and I am incredibly thankful that I am not sitting in front of him! I would be making the wrong assumption, as it's just Apolo training his mind to win another Olympic medal.

To understand how Apolo can cause beads of sweat to run down his face by using his mind, we have to start with the circumstances surrounding his on-ice training. Apolo made an observation early on in his career. Other teams were spending four hours training on the ice, but his team only had two hours. Why? The answer was less than ideal but not surprising—cost. His team could only afford two hours a day of ice time.

The limitation in training was one of the most critical points in his Olympic training. A choice was made by Apolo and his team to train with such intentionality and focus that two hours would yield four hours in results. The podium results confirm this, yet it was how Apolo described feeling during his races that caused me to lean into our conversation.

His training allowed him to perform and feel like he was "getting nothing but green lights." Apollo said, "The effort you're putting in doesn't seem like it's that much, it's just this perfect sweet spot between not trying hard enough and just trying hard enough." Apollo was no doubt in flow states where time slowed, and he was able to forecast where his opponents would be during the next lap while making critical decisions in microseconds. His mind and body were perfectly synchronized to perform at their best. This was only possible because of his highly focused and intentional mental and physical training.

If you are thinking, "This is not relatable to my life," given it's unlikely you are training for the Olympics (high fives if you are!), pause this negative narrative because you *can* make it relatable. We are all faced with constraints in life, things that are outside our control (see Ryan Holiday's profile), but we always have full autonomy over how we react to situations and the intentions we set.

Apolo took what was seen as a limitation to on-ice training and set an intention to fully show up during those two hours, to not waste a single minute, which allowed him to achieve world-class results in half the time. Apolo would arrive at the gym without any music blasting in his ears, a typical hack to motivate or pump us up when exercising. He wanted to be so focused on his training that he could feel and activate every fiber of his muscles being trained.

Think of the areas in your life where you would like to double the results in half the time.

We can all do this. It's not only reserved for Olympic athletes. If you only have twenty minutes to exercise today, make those twenty minutes as intense as someone working out for an hour. We can use the same approach to our mental training. For example, instead of speed reading a nonfiction book to check off a certain number of books for the year, try reducing the number and reading each page with focus and intention. Interact with the content and understand how the words on the page can help you in your life right now.

Do my practices support my ambitions?

While speed skating, Apolo often entered a flow state. But he was honest with me in saying, "I have yet to feel this physically since retiring, but what does translate is the mental component." Apolo knew his mental training was essential when competing, but he did not truly realize just how important it was until he stopped doing it. The days felt faster. The world was moving quicker. He felt more stressed, and he found himself reacting versus responding. Something needed to change. Apolo set the intention to get back to the basics.

He focused on four questions:

1. Am I moving well?
2. Am I sleeping well?
3. Am I eating well?
4. Am I thinking well?

We underestimate the basics, as Apolo realized, "When I do these things, it seems like all other things fall into place."

I don't think this is by accident. As humans, we tend to take simple things and make them more complicated. We have an endless amount of technology to track our health and habits, but are we any healthier? I'm a fan of technology, but I have to say Apolo made me think about focusing on the basics. If I feel tired, I go to sleep earlier. I don't need an app to tell me this.

Where can you simplify your thinking? When it's simple, we do it. When we do it, we get results. As Apolo says, "There are days I will just sit in my chair and breathe for 30 seconds." Imagine that! Breathing, the thing we all *have* to do but often ignore. Let's change this right now. Take in a long, deep breath, starting low in your belly, letting it travel all the way up to the top of your head— let it out slowly. Doesn't it feel amazing? Try starting off your morning with a few simple focused breaths, or do it at any point during the day when you feel stressed, overwhelmed, or out of control. Pausing for a few deep breaths will have a tremendous positive effect on the situation.

Am I setting Olympic-level reminders?

Life happens to us all, making it challenging to even keep up with the basics. That's why the most decorated American Winter Olympian of all time needs constant reminders. Are you ready for his Olympic-level reminder system? I want to introduce you to...the sticky note! It can't get more basic than this. It's also why his reminder system works.

Write down your intentions, goals, affirmations, and triggers to keep your mind in a motivated and driven state. This may seem obvious, but it's a critical point: stick them in places you frequent, spots that are part of your routine. If you have a coffee or tea ritual to start the day, put a reminder in this area.

As mentioned in Ryan Holiday's profile, I have his book *The Daily Stoic* leaning against my coffee machine. As the coffee pours, I am reading one passage to bring perspective to my life, think, and set the tone for my day. This is my version of the sticky note or reminder system. Remember the iPhone lock screen wallpaper trick I shared in Scott Belsky's profile? I see an affirmation, photo, or quote that I know positively triggers my mind each time I unlock my phone, which is my version of the sticky note. Find what works for you.

These reminders work. Have fun with them, get creative with the process, and remember to be kind to yourself. As Apolo reminded me, "There are times when I look at them and feel nothing, and there are times when I look at them and I remember why I wrote them." You may not always connect with your reminders, but trust that by consistently priming your mind you will form habits and systems to produce the life you desire.

Final Thought

Outworking your competitors starts with outworking yourself.

One Last Profile: My Own

As I write this, I cannot help but smile, thinking about how the entire journey unfolded for this book. At first, the idea of writing a profile on myself felt uncomfortable. Who am I to write a profile on myself? It feels narcissistic! The more I thought about it, the more I realized the clarity, focus, and excitement in my life right now resulted from the reflective methods outlined in *Personal Socrates,* and that my perspective could relate to others.

I reflected on a prompt that I often ask myself when considering whether or not to do something: *What's the worst that can happen?* The fear of being judged or not resonating with my profile held me back, but at the expense of someone finding value in my story. If I have learned one thing over the last decade of studying great minds, it's that it only takes one prompt or one perspective shift to completely alter our path.

I genuinely believe many of you will come out of my profile with a bulletproof end-of-the-year, or any-time-of-year, review system.

What do I want for my life?

This very question saved me, a question that paused and released an internal narrative that was sending me down a dark
path—a journey that felt hopeless, alone, and terrifying. This
question, by nature, is optimistic and progressive. I can't see
myself asking for a life of suffering and despair nor can I see
others asking for this life either. I released the narrative holding me back and answered the question based on what I wanted
in my life, not from a materialistic standpoint, but from how I
wanted my life to feel.

I set my intention, or my one-word theme, for the year:
Thriving. I will thrive in my thoughts, feelings, family, activities, health, and work. Spending time twelve months ago to set
this intention with goals, habits, and systems to support the intention has led to me being in a different headspace. Compared
to the introduction, I'm in an opposite place, one with a different set of questions, thoughts, and feelings.

Are all areas in my life thriving day in and day out? No, but
each day I am more clear, more intentional, and able to experience an expansion of possibility. This book, a move out of the
city and into nature, and working with exceptional people that
light me up each day have been my expansions that not long ago
would have seemed impossible. Yet, here I am, excited for new
possibilities to come—experiences, people, and circumstances
that I cannot predict but I know will unfold as I follow the signs
and breadcrumbs of life.

The question now becomes, what do I want for my life *now*?
In short, more of the same. As I write my profile, it's early December, a time when I start collecting my reflections from the

previous year and start planning conscious intentions for the upcoming year. To be clear, you can run this exercise at *any* point during the year. The flow is the same. I choose the end of the calendar year because the entire world slows down, making it even easier for me to slow down.

For those of you, like me, who like to know the practical details, I will explain my process. I credit a huge amount of my mental clarity to it, and I *now* know this process is firmly rooted in the Socratic method.

What did the last twelve months look like?

I always like to start by taking inventory of what actually happened over the last year, or in other words, I spend time getting clear. You can try and do this by memory, but unless you are superhuman, it will be challenging. Often the most prominent moments will come to mind first. Maybe this year you moved, changed jobs, ended a relationship; but there were other vibrant moments and events that most likely took place to appreciate and learn from as well. Here are three ways to do a high-level review of the year:

1. **Calendar scan:** Open up your calendar, go to the "view by month" option and scan the significant events, important meetings, vacations, and milestones you have recorded.
2. **Journal scan:** Open up your journal, do a quick scan of the things that stick out. The intent is not to reread everything you wrote, but to identify the "oh yeah, I forgot about that" moments.
3. **Photo scan:** Take out your phone, go back to the begin-

ning of the year, set up a month by month view and start scrolling. We are visual beings, so this scan often tells a great story and triggers many memories to reflect on.

Regardless of the method you use, list the moments that stand out so you can see everything in one glance. Now you can start unpacking what you learned and appreciated during those times, and also better understand what you want from your life.

Try out these prompts:

- What did I learn?
- What was amazing?
- What made me the happiest?
- What did I ignore?

Where can I be more focused and intentional?

Now, focus on painting a picture that supports your ambitions. Be intentional, and design a life that brings the feelings and emotions you want to live out each day. I find it helpful to pick a word or a theme for each year. As I mentioned earlier, my word for the year was "thriving." Pick something that speaks to you, and work through the prompts above to bring a clear picture of how you want the next twelve months to materialize.

Once you have a clear picture, you can then set goals and put systems in place to turn your vision into reality. I'm not going to dive into goal-setting practices, as countless books and articles are available to help in this process. I subscribe to the notion of setting clear goals and implementing robust systems to ensure my habits support the goals I have set out to achieve. If you want more on this subject, I suggest reading *Atomic Habits* by James

Clear or flip back to his profile as a guide.

The last step in the process is something I learned from best-selling author and world-class thinker Tim Ferriss. Take your plan and review each element from the perspective of what you would have to do to achieve each ambition in six months instead of twelve.

I know, it feels lofty. When I first heard about the tactic, I thought to myself, "Come on, I just spent all this time crafting a plan for the year, and now I have to restart on another timeline?" My original thinking was wrong. The intent is not to restart but to challenge your thought process and not settle on what intuitively comes to mind. Going a few layers deeper and challenging your initial thinking will open up a whole new path and set of opportunities.

Try out these prompts:

- Where do I want to be in the next twelve months?
- What steps do I need to take to get there?
- How does it look and feel when I get to that place?
- What are the affirmations that will help me?
- What can I do to achieve all of my ambitions in six months instead of twelve?

If you spend time with these prompts to get clear and intentional with your life, you will be pleasantly surprised by the opportunity presented to you. The feeling of waking up with a plan, a guiding light, and clear actions supporting your goals and desires make for beautiful days. Dream, explore, experiment, learn, and have fun with the process. If this practice speaks to you, do not wait until December to jump in. Run through the prompts and your reflection right now. I can say with certainty that you will come out the other side feeling motivated, driven, and alive!

Final Thought

Only a few minutes of intentional reflection can dictate months' worth of results.

Epilogue

Many prompts and practices have been shared. The objective is not to implement them all in one sitting, but to experiment with those that feel right to you right now. As your life evolves, so will the prompts and what feels relevant. Always follow your intuition, and let your reflection guide you.

Reflection is the difference between people staring from afar wondering why they do not have the legacy of a legend versus the world-class performers of today who work consistently to train their minds each day to reach the heights of the legends before them. It's a decision that will expand awareness, discipline, and dedication leading to a path of mastery and world-class performance.

The humans profiled in this book are just that—humans, like you and me. It's up to us to understand where we are now, where we want to be, and what actions to take next. I wish you nothing but a thriving mind that supports the life of your dreams.

Never forget: We are who we are because of the questions we ask or the questions we do not ask. You are always one question away from a completely different life. What is that question for you?

For book reference list visit baronfig.com/personalsocrates/references

What's Next?

I continue to collect and curate questions from remarkable humans and provide only the best prompts, along with my perspective, in a short and intentional email. If you'd like to continue expanding your mental fitness and reflection, you can sign up at:

baronfig.com/MarcChampagne

Acknowledgements

First, I must thank the world-class performers and legends featured in this book. Thank you for your time, energy, and wisdom. I can only hope that the ripple effect of your inspiration continues to reach more minds through the pages of *Personal Socrates*.

To every stunning human I've been fortunate to interview, the combination of your stories, practices, and reflective questions are what made this book possible. Thank you for your continued inspiration fueling my mind, and many others, each day.

To my remarkable wife Roxanne Champagne: Though I wrote the words, you lived the experience every step of the way. I could not ask for a better partner to make the journey of life with, and I look forward to our next adventure together. Thank you for always believing in me, and supporting everything I set my mind to. It means the world to me—I could not do it without you.

To my buddy and son Caleb Champagne, you may be too young to realize it, but your energy, curiosity, and countless smiles inspired and influenced many of the words in this book. Witnessing your mind develop has been a gift, and I can only hope that these pages find you when you are ready to consume them.

To my family, I am grateful for your unwavering support in anything I do. To my father-law, Mike Myre, who continues to guide me in finding *my questions*, pushing me to grow, and always serving as a reminder to cherish the details of life. To Josee Denison, my sister-in-law and number one fan of the Behind the Human podcast, your texts and support light me up—thank you!

To Sunay Shah, my brother-in-law and co-crazy-founder who took the plunge into the unknown with me to start KYO. This book wouldn't exist without our journey together; something I will never forget and always appreciate. To the KYO team, I am proud of what we accomplished together and thankful to have touched so many lives because of your dedication and passion.

Thank you Joey Cofone for believing in me and for publishing *Personal Socrates*. You are an incredible human with a stunning mind, and it's an honor to be on this journey with you. To the entire team at Baronfig, and especially Andi and Taylor for the early reads and feedback, and Jay for bringing this project to life, thank you for your energy and passion.

To James Clear, for providing priceless early advice and for introducing me to the legendary Peter Guzzardi. Peter, you are a magician of words and I thank you for your guidance and the confidence you ignited in me. To Ryan Holiday and Brent Underwood for pivoting this book into what it is today—you never know what one call can do. To Bruce Bowser for your writing advice, continued mentorship, and friendship.

To my editor, and at times writing therapist, Chantel Martin, you are a stunning human and I cannot imagine having gone through this experience without you. Your perfectly timed words of encouragement and inspiration to "just keep writing" were priceless. To the full team of copy editors, thank you for taking the manuscript to the finish line and for making me seem like I know how to write!

To my unofficial publishing lawyer and best friend Troy Asselin. Thank you for being part of every major moment in my life. To Steph and Josh, for being those friends who always have my back, supporting and cheering me on no matter what I do. I appreciate you beyond words.

To Nathan and the three Matts in my men's group, you helped me process the most challenging moments and emotions of my life while guiding me to find the clarity I was seeking. I will always be thankful to each of you (see Dan Doty's profile for more about this group).

To my dearest friend Jennifer Hansford, for once giving me an empty picture frame to fill with an image representing one of my biggest accomplishments. Jen, I will be printing the cover of this book and proudly displaying it in your frame. Thank you for the years of laughs, support, and love.

To my mom and dad, who raised me with nothing but love, support, and guided me in becoming the person I am today. Thank you, and I love you.

And, of course, to each of you who dedicated your time and energy in reading this book. Never stop upgrading your questions, and live the life you deserve.

About the Author

Marc Champagne unpacks the mental fitness practices and reflective questions shaping the lives of some of the most successful and brilliant thinkers in the world. He is the host of the top 50 podcast Behind the Human with 200+ interviews, and co-founder of the journaling app KYO, which ended up reaching close to 90 million people around the world. He has studied mental fitness practices for over a decade and has consulted for top-rated digital journals and wellness companies.

See more at behindthehuman.com

About Baronfig

Baronfig's mission is: To champion thinkers around the world through inspiration and imagination. They do this by creating tools for thinkers. What is a thinker? If you have thoughts, you're a thinker. Every human being engages their mind all day, every day. Literature expands knowledge, inspires ideation, and encourages conversation. From creating tools for thinkers, to imparting wisdom and knowledge to thinkers—Baronfig provides an ecosystem for thinkers to thrive.

See more at baronfig.com

Notes

Notes

Personal Socrates

Notes